MEDITATIONS

James R Warren

First Published in the United Kingdom in 2022 by Midland Tutorial Productions

First Edition 15 July 2022

Text copyright © James R Warren, 1997-2022
Photographs copyright © James R Warren 1997-2022
Acknowledged Photographs © Various Contributors
Diagrams © James R Warren 2022
Cover Design: James Warren

The right of James Randolph Warren to be identified as the author of this work has been asserted in accordance with the Copyright, Designs and Patents Act 1988

All rights reserved.

No part of this publication may be reproduced, stored or transmitted in any form or by any means (including photocopying or storing it in any medium by electronic means and whether or not transiently or incidentally to some other use of this publication) without the written permission of the copyright owner, except in accordance with the provisions of the Copyright, Designs and Patents Act 1988.

This book may not be lent, resold, hired out or otherwise disposed of by way of trade in any form of binding or cover other than that in which it is published, without the prior consent of the Publisher.

File Prefix Code: MEDITAT

A CIP Catalogue record for this book is available from The British Library

ISBN 978 1 7396296 3 2

Printed and Bound by IngramSpark

Midland Tutorial Productions Publishers
31 Victoria Avenue
Bloxwich
Walsall
WS3 3HS
United Kingdom

MEDITATIONS

An Album of Religious Essays

James R Warren

MIDLAND TUTORIAL PRODUCTIONS
BLOXWICH

To The Glory of The Loving God

Who Made Our Minds Free

TABLE OF CONTENTS

Page

PUBLICATION INFORMATION	V1
TITLE PAGE	R2
EPIGRAPH	5
TABLE OF CONTENTS	7

CHAPTER 1 *Exordium*

Exordium	11

CHAPTER 2 *Photographs for Meditations*

Photographs for Meditations	15

CHAPTER 3 *A New Condition*

The Convert	27
Explanatory Examination of "The Convert"	33
The Theurgist	39
The Infinite Unknowing	41
Things I Cannot Really Understand	45
More Things I Cannot Really Understand	47
Some Delightful Things	49
What is Justice?	51

CHAPTER 4 *Out and Beyond*

Jobs, Peace, Freedom	57
The Ambiguous World of Alexander Ivanov	61
Problems that Remain	69
Bunhill Fields	75
The Reprieve of War	83
Woman and Child in The Vision of Nicolas Poussin	85
The Tree of Snails	93
Children of God	99
Can Quakers Grasp the Nettle? An Attender Enquires	105
The Voyage of the Sigismondo	111
The Shining Embassy of Alopen	117
Catching Creatures	125
Sin	137
Why?	145
Eclipse in Mexico	147
Manumission	155
Perdition's Illusion	163
The Fishes of Rimini	171
Was Juniper a Woodentop?	177
The Road to Bedford Gaol	181
Arrested on King Street	183
A Light Outwith	187

CHAPTER 5 *Epilog*

How to Cherish	191

CHAPTER ONE

Exordium

8 December 2008

There is an old joke that I fear shall play on me in its fullest literality. When I was fifteen I knew everything and was amazed at the confusion and perplexity about me. When I went to university I found there were gaps in my knowledge but confidently considered that they would fill. When I was thirty I learned there was no possible system to subsume all knowledge, and when I was fifty I knew only that knowing was impossible. Now that I am seventy I appear to be reverting to the insouciance of infancy.

So what of that greater question: Can we know God?

Much has been written of the Sea of Faith since Arnold mourned its withdrawal as his wife and he heard it roar away in the Dover night. For me, my faith in Christ is a great exploration where remarkable discoveries, and even strange new creatures, beset every prospect. Balboa knew he beheld a new sea, and Newton combed his beach beside an ocean he knew he could not navigate, but it lies to us to contemplate a great expanse of inscrutability, refulgent and sublime, eternal yet of no time, serene and strewn with the wreckage of libraries.

There is no art of man; scientific, doctrinal or philosophical which can define reality, for all systems consummate in contradiction and incompleteness. All we can do is live, love, trust, believe and strive to know Our Savior personally, you may say subjectively, so that at the end we may say, not I know this or I found that: But "I have been there, done that, got the tee-shirt".

It is important to remember that The Cross is about the transcendence of suffering and that we are suffering together. I try to remember to pray not only for my human family and friends but also for the waterfowl, rats, squirrels and other small creatures I see about. For they suffer and yet are innocent of evil, so if indeed there is The Resurrection of the Flesh then assuredly these last shall be first.

The Conception of Existence

Both the Existence of God and the non-existence of god are logically impossible. But the former is, on balance, the more probable, and certainly the more congenial.

The Life that God begat is very unlikely indeed, but apparently here.

If that life is not an involuntary emanation of His Thought then even larger and more disturbing questions arise.

And if the genesis of matter was virtually instantaneous then the implication is that its annihilation is also a summary event.

Notwithstanding my indefinite discursion you can safely take it from me that God exists, that we are continuing to frustrate His best efforts, and that He is keeping His eye on us.

Life is a campaign activity. Its costs are often exorbitant and ultimately total. We should respect the life we have been lent, as we cherish the lives of the creatures about us.

To despise life is an insult to God and a repudiation of His ideas. To despise life is cruelty and cruelty brings sin. Christians believe that our sins are forever reprieved of our recompense in Hell by the final and sufficient Sacrifice of Our Holy Savior. Notwithstanding this, you suffer in this life the guilt, hate and alienation your cruelties bring. You strive to forgive yourself and for the forgiveness of those you value, and you look to a better future.

I am almost certainly more evil than you. I too seek forgiveness of God and man. I should pray for your forgiveness and your spiritual refreshment. I should hope you pray for mine.

The human mind coheres aspects of the animal and the Divine. The problem is that God is not an animal, at least not in any sense comprehensible to a human or his collective. There is an existential mismatch.

Part of the problem is simply that His thoughts are not our thoughts. (This is not my idea: It says so in The Bible). This is not a failing of God, neither a spite of any agent. The difficulty resides with human beings. It arises from natural limitations upon the intellectual power that we can focus on problems.

To refuse the image for the word is a fatal error, for to prefer the symbol to the res represented is the antithesis of reason. The fathers put aside the naked and the nude, and soothing scenes of tranquil pastures, as supposed idolatry. Minds focused upon the text rather than its Meaning, a sign of madness. The image of the real was clothed in the vacancy of limewash, or, even more disastrously, with geometrical patterning, as if to raise the genius of Euclid higher than the immanence of God.

To refuse the reality for the image is a fatal error, for to prefer the likeness to the res represented is the antithesis of nature. The Moderns put aside the painful and insanitary immediacies of experience and focused upon the picture and its schema rather than its object, a sign of evasion. The image of the real was invested with a film of glossy abstraction, or, even more disastrously, a specious aura of definitive veracity, as if to raise the idealisations of Leonardo above the fabric of Creation.

The virtues of the European Enlightenment: Trust, Humaneness, Naturalism, and Reason brought us very far but can go little further without supplement. Reason is a luxury of the leisured. Human beings quite simply are not rational, for if they were they would never have evolved, and would hardly have been made irrational by a Creator. If they were rational they certainly would not do anything inimical to individual or collective survival. By the first half of the Nineteenth Century it was already clear to advanced thinkers, both in mathematics and philosophy, that people needed something extra.

What is truth? Does truth inhere in the blueprint of intended perfection that includes unknown errors of guidance, or in the consummated effect whose defects are latent or manifest? Or does truth inhere in the spirit of entropy who disrupts the realisation? Quakers talk of speaking truth to power, but the nature of each remains largely unexplored, and the interaction of the two almost unappreciated. Bacon was wrong. Pilate made no jest. And Our Holy Savior knew an explanation would take a very long time. If the Roman had stayed for his answer the two men would still discourse upon The Gabbatha, and a world would remain unedified.

For evil can be confuted by no dialectic, and yet evil is vincible, because suffering can be turned to good effect.

I believe that there is some sense of meaning in which God made the world, and living things are a spawn of his consciousness. But His historical behaviour shows that our condition grieves him and that he is ready to attempt improvements where he can, and in particular where we let him. If God really were Almighty then Paradise would be ubiquitous. I am not saying we control God. That would be absurd. I am saying there is such a thing as Free Will. We can freely choose good or evil, for ourselves and for those under our power.

I hope that you enjoy this selection of my religious writings and I hope they stimulate you further to contribute your own theories and experiences to this limitless, and most perilous, of all reconnaissances. But most of all I hope they inspire you to fly closer to The Feet of Salvation, whether by a picometer or a parsec.

This is for you. Enjoy.

CHAPTER TWO

Photographs for Meditations

14 December 2008

HOWARD1gammaundistreclones.jpg
Castle Howard
am 28 March 1997
SE715700
At noon on that Good Friday I entered the house and found Christ.

THRONEB4clones.jpg
The Throne of St Peters, The Vatican, Rome
February 1979

XPFIG4Fclones.jpg
The Crucifixion as a Memorial to the Great and Falklands Wars
St Peter's Church, Walsall
am 21 September 2006
SP010994
The Loveliest Image of Christ I have seen. By an unknown artist.
The Dedication reads:-

> IN HONOUR OF
> ## THE SAVIOUR OF THE WORLD
> AND IN PIOUS MEMORY OF THE MEN OF THIS CHURCH AND
> PARISH WHO LAID DOWN THEIR LIVES IN THE GREAT WAR
> THIS SYMBOL OF THE MYSTERY OF REDEMPTION
> WAS DEDICATED JULY 27TH 1919
>
> GREATER LOVE HATH NO MAN THAN THIS THAT A MAN
> LAY DOWN HIS LIFE FOR HIS FRIENDS

DSBUTTS1clones.jpg
The Dedication Stone
The Butt's Primary School, Marlow Street, Walsall
am 6 November 2001
SP001994
The Dedication reads:-

> IN HONOUR OF THE RISEN CHRIST
> AND IN OBEDIENCE TO HIS COMMAND
> TO "FEED THE LAMBS" OF HIS FLOCK
> THIS SCHOOL WAS ERECTED IN THE
> YEAR OF OUR SALVATION 1913

Postscript: 12 June 2022

By 1998 I found the school already closed and it was demolished circa 2005-10. The whereabouts of the pink granite dedication stone is not known to me.

SIGIS1clones.jpg
The Motor Ketch "Sigismondo" at San Vincenzo Pier
Stromboli
Evening 27 May 1998

BLAKE2uprights.jpg
The Grave of William Blake
Bunhill Fields
London
am 13 September 2007
TQ327823

STEVWEL1s.jpg
The Holy Well, Stevington
pm 8 April 2001
SP990536
Adverted to in John Bunyan's "Pilgrim's Progress", and in "The Road to Bedford Gaol". Visited with my Wife Jana.

CHAPTER THREE

A New Condition

The Convert

2-29 June 1997

In the Beginning was The Word
And the Word was Love
And Love moved over the Face of the Deep
Whose chill darkness reflected the Light above

Full lonely the moping Love did weep
For a mate in the wastes of Her desolate space
Full copiously Her sweetwater tears did steep
The impassive salt main of that primal place

And then was a Male by her smile beguiled
That surprised succeeded as tears did cease
And Love married Honor and bore Him a child
Whose jubilant parents called it Peace

Why baptise in a teeming torrents slack kiers
In the flowing spates of the spring melt clear?
When only your hot streaming saline tears
Can cleanse your soul to Christ so dear

For then Justice jaded of m'ludding
Of Law's stripes and strokes made pursy
Dallied with green Hope abudding
Whose sacred fruit of joining they called Mercy

Blessed is the Quest for Love
For the Lover shall leave the pit of strife
And his tears of joy will season his soul
For the meek content of Eternal Life

Blessed is the brightly Rising Light
Which suffuses the City of Kindling Dawn
For it shall scatter the Doubts of Night
Discover the paths to the Capitol Crown

The Law proscribed the gift of death
Yet the Law itself has deceased rather
For whilst the Law maintained its breath
It forbore to banish the Wrath Death's father

Now in this still and pregnant morn
The listless winds of change bestir
The ancient mortal World reborn
Turns the apogee of Hope's nadir

For now the wild etesian storm
Howling round the braes of Being
Showers the balmy water warm
In aspersion of Pride's slave afreeing

    Prince of Life, I hear Your Call
    I hasten to Your Light of Love
    Open my Eyes, my Lies forestall
    Lift my Mind to That Above

    I peer down the dark well shaft
    To the twinkling pool below
    I cannot reach by mortal craft
    The saving draught to life bestow

    Surge aloft the living water
    Burst on me the cleansing fount
    Pour on me Your clement Quarter
    With lucid force my sins surmount

    Strip my clinging sordid cover
    And let me bathing naked bask
    In prayer my slaking Soul discover
    My killing sins with You unmask

    In the mighty tumbling plume
    Lest neath the Purity I sink
    In the driven spray and spume
    Lend me the wondrous Source to drink

    Let the fitful desert breeze

Anoint me in the scorch of noon
With drifting chrism of the trees
That in their blooming fragrance swoon

Let the Relict me revest
Lead me through the darnel mown
To the waving wine-blond harvest
Of the Bounty You have sown

As you disclaimed Your Holy Powers
Ceding Honor to Your Sire
Strike down my high and prideful towers
Your strength is all that I require

Let me pass Your Love to others
Quench away my flaming ire
Break with me and all Your Brothers
The Endless Feast of fair desire

Let us walk upon the water
On its firm rock-calm substrate
With Love's refreshing daughter
Pace its pure and clean estate

Through the glodes the sunbeams glimmer
Dappling agrestal silent pitches
As the aspen poplars shimmer
In the vespertinal cool

The shock of squalls' affusion
Trains the unkempt foulway grasses
In their late vernal profusion
By the unrowed boating pool

The abele and willow sprays
Glaucously abask and tremble
In the slanting aurous sun rays
On the poolside monticule

To the glistening concrete pavement
Beyond the rippling lakelet's glare

Arrives a father and his infant
In a rusting small pushchair

Rests the young man on a park-bench
And lifts his son with tenderness
Folds the calash with a wrist wrench
Reft of men and womanless

Gently settles he the infant
At his feet whilst he adjusts
The rain-drenched calash quadrant
Against the fitful vernal gusts

Magnolias' candid calyces
Bloodstreaked in votive lambency
Fall to the caress of the breeze
In quivering fleshly cadency

Chase in rout the wounded petals
Across the springing lightening lawn
Steadfastly cling the shy green sepals
To greet the splendor of the dawn

Upon the pavement lands a nut
Out darts a squirrel with surprise
His fluffy frame and flouncing scut
Delights the baby's fearless eyes

Ascends the child from his seating
And toddles at the tiny beast
Absconds the rodent fast and fleeting
With his free and tasty prize

Stumbles on the cadet walker
As his dad he fascinates
Raptured squeaks the trainee talker
Towards a cold watery demise

From his rapt and riant stupor
Leaps the father for the brink
Leaps to catch his darling stumbler
Ere forever he does sink

Gently is the infant caught
And kissed in arms of tearful strength
With cries is Father's succor sought
Cuddling confirms the filial link

Slowly folds the disused stroller
Then hand in hand the two depart
Each to else a saved consoler
A dearly warm and solaced heart

Across the rolling golfing links
They amble through the gathering dusk
Before the setting sunlight sinks
And lamp and leaving lane do part

Soon they reach the alameda
Whose alate flanks repulse the squall
Which Southward drives the plumose poplar
Flexing like a yielding wall

Son and Sire are sheltered both
Beneath the spread alerion
From the driving hailstorm wroth
Between the fields Cimmerian

And as the stinging pelt decamps
The whispering boughs rebound
And livid files of vapor lamps
Strike arcs to light the ground

Beyond the glacilely-lined avenue
The man shoulders his tired young lad
As in the blue gloom they squint to construe
A ghostly figure silent and sad

As they near to her they shortly perceive
Around a cool and marmoreal calm
The clinging folds of a light cotton weave
Like a chilling ablative ihram

Briskly approach they the shivering maid
The young man enfolds her with his warm coat
Gently embracing the slight slender shade
With the promise and solace of psalm

Her large and lovely saxe eyes lift to his
As a sunrise smile of thanks greets his gaze
For the life-giving grace beyond riches
In silent communion of charm

Tenderly takes she the tiny toddler
And he snoozes back to the town
Contently with the kind coddler
In the corporal arms of no wraith

And Trust the father of Progress in life
Then forsook the forlorn death of the waif
And took vivified Patience to wife
And begat the sibling they styled Faith

An Explanatory Examination
Of "The Convert"

26 July 1997

By The Author, James R Warren

"The Convert" is a rhyming poem of forty-four quatrains divided into three cantos.

This analysis examines the text using the techniques of literary criticism, for the poem is a free-standing artistic creation, susceptible of secular description. The social and ethical principles implicit are doubtless common to many faiths as well as several humanistic lifestyles, honestly pursued. The theological content is the product of routine exegesis using The Authorised King James Version of The Holy Bible. Because of the many Scotticisms and rare Americanisms included a normal English dictionary is of limited assistance: I recommend the use of "Chambers English Dictionary".

The poem allegorically explores the antecedents and emotions of conversion to Christianity in terms of Gospel revelations. The Gospels relate the Words and Deeds of Christ. The three former Gospels (Matthew, Mark and Luke) are textually very similar and emphasise the ethical teaching of Christ. Matthew is perhaps the most comprehensive and literary and may in many contexts represent all three of these "Synoptic Gospels". The Gospel of St John is entirely different: It explores the nature of Salvation. The Apostolic Thesis is that Salvation is an individual's recompense for embracing the ethical ideals. The concept of Salvation does not of necessity depend upon a belief in the afterlife because it can equally be imagined as a sane and happy peace-of-mind in this life, the converse of the frustration, neurosis and anxiety which blight wrong-living. Accordingly the concept of Eternal Life, may be symbolic with little eschatological significance, though many Christians take the Promises of Christ at face value. I became a believer in the Living Immanence of Jesus Christ in middle age.

The first canto of ten stanzas has loose scansion commencing in iambic pentameter and changing to trochaic tetrameter at its conclusion. Whilst scripturally-based it makes much play of pagan concepts of begat virtue and expresses the confused inchoacy of the mind turning to Christ.

The second "prayer canto" also of ten stanzas is a fast-paced and powerfully-developed appeal to Christ in strict trochaic tetrameter, and naturally has a repentant Christian flavor. It is printed in Century rather than the narrative Courier of the rest of the poem.

The third canto of twenty-four stanzas starts in a galloping trochaic tetrameter but concludes in a decelerated iambic pentameter. This canto is wholly modern and Romantic in treatment exploring the care of God for Man in symbolic visual terms.

The entire piece of artwork therefore has a tripartite "symphonic" structure.

The First Canto

The opening stanza adapts John 1:1 which itself echoes the imagery of Genesis 1:2 as the ordering and reconciling principle of Divine Love surpasses the cold and barren sea of pointless self-divorce from Grace. God is identified with Love in His genitive and restorative beatitudes of Gen 1:22, 1:28 and 2:3. In this slightly pagan and androgynous phase, however, Love must play the mate of Honor if anything is to come of the situation. Studies have shown that only 16% of Christian converts are interested in reaching heaven (or evading hell). Rather it is their love of goodness whether latent or exogenous which turns them, combined with self-disgust. But those who have no honor are incapable of disgusting themselves. Thus Love and Honor can, given the right "thermodynamic" environment, react to produce the emotional peace (or if you prefer, leisure-of-mind) from which a considered change of direction can be decided.

The fourth stanza reflects the work of The Baptist in John 1:29-33 but clearly, as Christ often took pains to explain, purely formal initiations or observances cannot constitute Conversion, which is a radical behavioural change. If you are to repent and alter your ways you are going to do a lot of crying and enjoy a very strange and pleasant suffering.

Love and Honor get married before having Peace, but in the fifth stanza of our pagan exordium Justice and Hope have a very casual liaison whose result is by definition illegitimate. Justice demands fair and equitable retaliation in kind in human law but ignores the Divine hope of atonement with reconciliation and reconstruction, until it risks a leap in the dark and embraces that Hope. Throughout the Sermon on the Mount and especially in Matthew 6:14-15 and 7:2 Christ admits God's "mistake" in handing-down the Decalog and promulgates the antinomian manifesto of radical forgiveness which sets aside the brutal but sterile evolutions of The Law. So Mercy is a lovely bastard.

Stanzas Six and Seven based upon the Beatitudes of Christ (Matthew 5:7-11) and also Matthew 5:13, 5:14-16 develop the imagery of dawning enlightenment on the higher hillcrests of the soul.

Stanza Eight explicitly adverts to The Savior's admonition not merely to refrain from violating The Sixth Commandment but not even to call a man "thou fool" as this sets in train the gathering interplay of anger and violence which consummates in killing (Matthew 5:21-22).

The final two quatrains advert to Christ's dialog with Nicodemus concerning the Winds of Change and rebirth not only of water (baptism) but of The Spirit (conversion) (John 3:8).

The Second Canto

This brisk prayer commences by affirmation of Christ as The Prince of Life (Acts 3:15) a living god and God of the living (Mark 12:27). The convert wants to love and to learn: He yearns for both inexpressibly. (I frequently lie out of a lazy desire not to have to explain things to others, though I hope never through malice or fraud: However, I was not aware of *any* dishonesty until I turned to Christ).

A modern convert turns to Christ when *all* of his personal and social problem-solving resources have been tried and have failed.

Chapter Four of The Gospel of St John largely describes Christ's interview with the Samaritan Woman at The Well of Sychar in which He asks her for a drink of water and tells her that one who drinks of the well will thirst again but those who drink of the water of Divine Grace will never thirst again. Christ impresses her by discerning that she has had five husbands but is currently living with a man to whom she is unmarried. This most controversial of parables seems to develop Christ's antinomian prospectus and possibly allegorises the obsolescence of the Pentateuch.

The Convert can see what he wants but cannot reach it on his own. So Christ comes to him with saving Power and affuses him with cleansing Grace. Several Johannine verses (4:14, 3:5 and 4:6) are helpful with this text. Many converts speak of ecstasies in which they sense cold water pouring through their bodies or being bathed in warm oil. I have not experienced this, only feeling a sensation of warm and delightful security. Interestingly, I had not read of these fountain-like experiences when I wrote these stanzas.

The seventh stanza of this prayer alludes to the harvest of the damned and the saved discussed in Matthew 13:24-31 and John 4:7 and 4:35.

The "Relict" is at one level the Samaritan Woman but allegorises the empowering Word of The New Testament which Christ and his Apostles have bequeathed to posterity, and which teaches the Way of personal ethical Salvation with or without life after death.

Verse Eight alludes to Christ's confession of mere agency (John 5:30) in His Powers: And the Convert's renunciation of self-will in favor of Christ's guidance.

The penultimate stanza alludes to the self-generative and propagative nature of Love as one of only two desirable commodities not subject to Laplacian constraints and the natural laws of conservation. The old Aramaic writers explained this theme in terms of the "miracles" of the loaves and the fishes of which John 6:5-14 may serve as the type. Theologically, this helps to consolidate the status of Love as the supernatural progenitor.

The last verse of the prayer canto is an obvious allusion to Matthew 14:25-33 in which the Convert invites Christ to help him achieve the impossible: Forgive old enemies and, as in my case, literally shake hands with them.

The overall theme is the cleansing of sin, the extirpation of the past and a new beginning in Christ.

The Third Canto

Christianity is not relevant today if it is only conceivable in terms of Roman mythology and the "primitive" beliefs of Iron Age tribesmen who skulked around the margins of the Augustan Empire.

The last canto attempts to develop the Work of Christ in a modern setting but retains the metaphorical tradition.

It is a blustery spring afternoon in which a single parent wheels his little boy through the municipal park with a pushchair. The man represents The Son of Man who now has care and custody of the Convert, personified by the little boy. We are not told why the man is unemployed or why his wife has left him. All we need to know is that, though preoccupied, he will give timely and individual Love to his newborn. The most common emotion amongst converts of any age is that they feel like babies who are being softly cradled in the loving arms of a metaphysical Father.

The first three stanzas set the scene with a painterly and largely secular Romantic depiction of sunshine and showers over the golf course. The wind and sun play upon the gray-green foliage of the ornamental trees. (An abele is a white poplar and I had never knowingly seen one when I wrote this: Hence my interest in the likely abeles discovered beside the new Mill of Monquoich by-pass).

The pair rest beside the boating pool whilst dad attempts to fold the plastic awning over the pushchair. The baby, who cannot yet walk for himself is set aside during the operation. The pushchair is a prosthetic which has seen better days and is about to drop to bits, like the convert's ability to solve his problems from his own unaided resources.

Stanzas Seven and Eight use the ornamental magnolias shedding their petals nearby to represent the Flesh and Blood of Christ shed to redeem men. The flesh and blood falls and is gone, though it will appear again in due season. Meanwhile, Hope (whose traditional color in European iconography is green) clings to the firmly-planted bush awaiting better times.

Stanzas Nine, Ten and Eleven see the child rise and walk for the first time using his own legs though dad brought him to this place. The convert thinks that he wants the squirrel who is representing any vain but beguiling object of desire. But the desideratum promptly vanishes like a mirage, taking his own Salvation with him. The squirrel is cash, fame, wisdom, status, personal talent, what you will.

In Stanza Twelve Christ is so delighted to see his new son begin to walk in His Power that He briefly overlooks the imminent danger to which the Convert is consigning himself along the trajectory to Death.

But the next verse sees Christ catch the errant and kiss away his tears with smiling reassurances. I am of course well aware that a natural father is more likely to spank his lad than do that, or give him a clip round the ear. But The Savior cannot have anything which the universe contains taken away from him and therefore has no need to defend his own or to make any kind of point.

Verse Fourteen sees Father and son loving each other very much after their nasty fright and the final pensioning-off of the pushchair of self-will.

Verses Fifteen through Eighteen use imagery from the fifteenth-century devotional classic "The Imitation of Christ" by Thomas A'Kempis, who wrote of The Light of Christ illumining The Way to Salvation and also The Light of Christ shining beneath His spread eagle's-wings sheltering the devotee. Father and son exit the park by way of an alameda (a promenade lined with Lombardy poplars) whose gracile ranks are compared with the flight feathers of an eagle sheltering the pair from the blasts outwith. Beyond the sheltering wings are now-dark fields haunted by the unconverted. (In Ancient Rome the Cimmerii were a fabulous tribe who lived in a land of perpetual darkness). As the beating hail ceases the blue light of the mercury-arc lamps suffuses the avenue. (Blue represents fidelity and faith iconographically). The Light of Faith supersedes the storm of doubt through the Grace of God. Further iconography relates The Gospel of St Matthew, an essentially ethical document conventionally symbolised in art by a Man, to the subsumptive and superseding Gospel of St John, usually symbolised by the Eagle of transcendence.

Verses Twenty to Twenty-Four, developed in a slow iambic, describe the meeting of Father and Son with Patience, personified as a suffering and starved young woman. (Starved in both the ancient and modern senses: Freezing cold and hungry). Her pale blue eyes represent peace iconographically and The Son of Man warms and comforts her, lending motive power to accompany Savior and saved through the rest of their journey. But their daughter is Herself Faith, because turning to Christ is a risk-fraught Act of Faith instantiated as reconciliation with one's enemies as well as impersonal aspects of private vulnerability, and that turning itself engenders Faith. The Son of Man needs Patience to support his ongoing Fatherhood: The Convert needs his Sister to support him.

The Theurgist

6-7 August 1997

Care we for His pedigree
Since children are begat in joy?
Regard instead the majesty
That kindly Powers His hands deploy

Remember that in desert drought
His Sacred Spirit spurned the stones
And put the Siren Self to rout
That glutton lust the corpse enthrones

Why deify the transient flesh?
The ravens feed and yet soar free
Harvest not and do not thresh
And still the golden dawn they see

Slept He upon the heaving sea
Yet heard His Servants' cries of fear
Before the waves heard his decree
He told the souls to admit cheer

Upon the reeling seething main
Uttering words of gentle balm
Reproved the winds and lashing rain
Restoring then a Halcyon calm

Then on the pending slopes about
He found oppressed the tomb-bound pair
Cast out their demons with a shout
Their tortured heads did he repair

He cured the wench by blood defiled
When bidden by the chieftain come
And raised from death the cooling child
And cured the faithful blind and dumb

A lad He raised from out the dead
At the seventh hour of light
And sent the happy father sped
To the hearth of his delight
At the bubbling pool Bethesda
Sick men waited on the seething
Loitered in the cool exedra
To ease their fevered labored breathing

To he who longed but could not
Bathe pre-empted by the agile
He told to raise his lifeless cot
And leave the cloister mobile

In Siloam bathed He the eyes
Of the blind who then did see
With limpid grace which clarifies
From turbid sin he set him free

Jesus wept and Jesus groaned
But Jesus rolled away the stone
And he that was for four days dead
Healed arose his stony bed

Jesus wash my hands and head
As You washed the souls You led
Show me that to wisely lead
Is to love and answer need

The Infinite Unknowing

14 January 2011

Why should we baulk at the contradiction of the laws of science in a universe created by a careless God who knew neither necessity nor convention? Why so? Is science just a shorthand appellation for our provisional ideas of what we surmise at this time? We smile at telepathy, but accept radio as commonplace.

In a universe of infinite temporal and spatial extent coeval with an infinity of infinite spaces even the least probable thing must be a certainty: Somewhere today a troupe of monkeys shall collaboratively compose the entire oeuvre of Shakespeare, just as surely as the scattered bones shall rise and walk. Why did The Holy Office find this idea so repugnant that they would burn a man for it?

That man taught us that ideas are only the shadows of truth. And yet in an infinite world among numberless worlds all is true, and where all is true time and space loses its meaning. A very devout man he asserted the essential irrationality of his Christian religion. We might put it like this: Reason is the great discriminator, and where all is true there is no fallacy, and reason gains no purchase.

Reason is a derivative product of intelligence, an instinct that continuously optimises the probability of its possessor's survival.

Perverted reason affords the delights of speculation, whether in science love or exchange.

But reason has these limits and no relevancy beyond the animal.

A mathematician or scientist has to accept an argument for Divine Existence when the evidence for rational intentionality in the progress of our world is more probable than its negation, even whilst aware that the very concept of probability is meaningless in the presence of infinity, and that thought itself is fallible.

And a geologist is trained to doubt the integrity of the very ground on which he stands, knowing that evolution and decay are artefacts of chance.

If there was a Big Bang it must have had a volitional agent of antecedence who stood somewhere to select his place and time? If there is

Steady State then infinite time and space is a here-present reality and God exists because all must.

If the World is voluntary is it Good or Evil, or are these virtues mere chimeras that die with us, or are survival stratagems?

It will not do to attempt proof of the autonomy of systems by reference to the Dawkins Weasel or some other paradigm of selection. As has been pointed-out by others such experiments require a finite end-point, and therefore a pre-specified perfection. For such simplified and purely symbolic schema, Gödel proved eighty years ago that no language could be sufficiently complete to express all possible messages, and we have been invited to extend this finding to material structures coded in quarks and photons or something.

We are forced to confront the evil hour at which a mature appraisal is required. And yet find ourselves on the horns of another quandary, knowing that all human decision is error, including Euclid's Parallel Postulate and all judicial verdicts ever. We are unqualified due to the finite extent of intellect, and its own finite existence, which ensures that human thought can never have the last word.

So all proof is error.

I am a Mercian, a native of central England. In my country people have big problems with Creation and with any concept that touches upon creativity. These things are confounded by both the intellectuals and the laity with manufacturing, the arts, labor and handicraft, all of which are considered dishonorable. To associate any such activity with The Godhead is considered almost blasphemous. This anti-labor view has powerfully promoted the ascendancy of atheism in my culture.

You will probably take the contrary view that all these material skills or productions are very laudable, and that in any case The Work of God is ontologically distinct.

We cannot of course delineate the Program of God, and we barely discern it. Indeed it is very difficult to analyse our own creative acts in anything but outline.

I will have a go at a very superficial description of a general creative program:-

(a) Selection

The first and most primitive desideratum of a creative act is to survey the promiscuous chaos of all visible things and pick out the items needed.

A philatelist might content himself with the search and selection of only the Europa designs for the many thousands of postage stamp designs printed. He recognises that whilst this is a finite set of a finite universe he cannot arrogate each extant example and must content himself with a specimen of each type, and even then resigns himself to knowing that some varieties will ever elude him.

(b) Arrangement

A selection of requisite things having been gathered it remains to arrange them. There are usually many, or often many milliards, of possible arrangements, some of which may be useful or handsome.

The busy bowerbird selects his treasures from the forest floor, choosing only the most lustrous jewels and the most curious exotica to garnish his grotto. Never content with mere possession he forever re-arranges his gains the more affectingly to beguile any lady who may visit. A discerning, discrete and industrious bird who has luck on his side will at last bed his bride amidst the sparkling splendor of his resplendent materials. No antiquary of The Rococo ever lavished more love or labor upon his cabinet, or gained such satisfaction therefrom.

Consider also the carpenter. He wishes to make a table and has already selected from the infinite array of available things four legs and a wooden board. He spurned all the legs of antelope, of journeys, and of pylons that hove to mind as well as the various boards of directors, of lodgings, and of intercalated ignimbrites, for he adjudged these and other things ill-fitted to his intent.

He now needs to arrange these components, and is presented with many, perhaps infinite, possibilities.

Perhaps he might fit a leg to three of the board's corners, and the fourth as a reinforcing truss across a selected pair. You may think that eccentric, but it makes right good sense if the tabletop board is triangular. Or if the board is rectangular he may fit legs to adjacent corners, and the other two as supportive strakes on the board face. Methinks it is like an easel.

The possible permutations of even the most judiciously selected components exceed the wit of both birds and men.

(c) Optimisation

We now come to the most problematic of our perplexing scheme of creation, the part that has most stressed the followers of Malthus and Darwin (believers both) as well as the proponents of Divine Design: The making of our assembled product as good as it can be.

Good for which purpose, and good for how long?

If fitness has no purpose and is only fleeting then by what measure is it fit?

There are certain mathematical artefacts that are of an approximate character, that approximate the same thing, and yet are in some sense mutually incompatible and mutually incapable of perfection. Examples are the Ptolomaic, the Newtonian and the Einsteinian conceptions of cosmic reality.

Yet what is perfection and where is the common criterion that enables us the judge the aptitude of systems?

Things I Cannot Really Understand

12 October 1997

Is it not strange that I who have written so much so often about things he thought he understood should choose on this lovely sunny Autumn afternoon to discourse upon things he does not really understand?

But life is full of paradox.

The Ancients warned us of this with their strange logical and mathematical contradictions so clear to posit and yet so refractory of decision. And yet it is not the paradoxes that I remember, but the names of their titular authors as if the riddles were no more than the ghosts of departed chimeras. For are these old conundra any more than guardians at the gates of greater understanding like the Cerberus chained safely to stay in three minds about whether to bark, to guard or to slay? Or perhaps they are kindly durwards no more repulsive or exclusive than the commissionaire of reason who delays, reproves and gently points the way to unlooked-for possibilities.

Why is it, and how can it be, that the Friends forgather in silence the better to laud their God, and deepen that silence into the noiseless joy of weeping as their Witness raves and rages about them, so that the stranger fears for the safety of his hearing?

How was it that my constant friends deserted me when I most needed them, saying they would lie to protect their own jobs, when all my enemies rallied around me whether to prey, avenge or save? And how could these disorganised and undirected men, with their private and profane agendas, have led me to the Salvation of Christ?

No argument could have convinced and no proof converted, for arguments are flawed, proofs for ever doubted, and all imperatives could have their counterclaim. Only the most tenuous of casual coincidences could have caused the certainty of Faith.

What price Godel, Heisenberg, Einstein? The world of Men is finite and they have proven it by confronting the limitless. The shell of a snail measures the order of ratio and proportion in the subtlest Phidian scheme, and shares with the sunflower the evolution of the bounded from the transcendental. And yet these creatures, we must presume, remain innocent of these things as they pass their haywire commerce across my garden.

In the First Book of Corinthians Paul tells us that it pleased God by the foolishness of preaching to save them that believe; that the Greeks seek after wisdom and that to them Christ Crucified is foolishness; but that the foolishness of God is wiser than men. And that whilst the Greeks seek after wisdom the Jews require a sign.

George Cantor was a Jew. He knew several things about signs and possibly a little wisdom. He achieved the impossible by counting the indenumerable and finding several flavors of infinity. Yet George Cantor was not God. Jesus was a Jew, a God and a Man and told us that whilst some things were impossible with men, all things were possible with God. Why then did God rescue the souls of men by sending his own Son to sacrifice?

More Things I Cannot Really Understand

17 October 1997

Am I a Dualist? What is a Dualist? What is Duality? How can I ask this when I have not even discerned The Monad?

Huygens was a very clever man who said that Light was a train of waves. Newton was a very clever man who said that it was a stream of corpuscles. The ship is a corpuscle that moves over the waves. But where does the wave end and the thing begin? We are invited to believe that even this large particle has a small but finite De Broglie wavelength through which it oscillates between the real and the merely potential.

Young seemed to have settled the argument with the Diffractive Interference of Light, for what stream could diffract, notwithstanding the erratic adhesions of jets leaving orifices? And yet doubt lingered to be rekindled by Einstein and his photoelectricity.

Is Christ both Divine and Human? Do we know what is Divine? Do we know what is human? Is a snail human? He has not Fallen and needs no Salvation. Is he accordingly Divine?

Is it the case that though controversy may rage between The School of That and The School of This that both discern The Truth but in Its differing aspects like the refractive fire of the dispersive diamond as its facets meet The Light at this attitude and then the other?

Reverting to the snail. I saw him patrol my driveway in the darkness of an Autumn evening. I saw him have Sacred Communion with his wife. I say "him" for my conservative mind set. It may have been her. But I am told that a snail may engage its sex at will for now begetting as the man for then bearing as the wife. Have I missed something or have I apprehended a deeper secret of our being?

If I am feminine do I partake of the masculine? If I am made in The Image of God then am I cast in The Mask of Evil?

The Gospel of John opens by declaring God to be The Word and The Light, but we limited and finite creatures see The Word as purely semiotic and Light as purely physical. For sure we ascertain that no message can propagate without the physical agent, as no physical entity may cohere without the ordering principle. But do we with the Ancients dichotomise these elements or can they be integrated and assimilated to The One?

If I embrace The Light Within must I reject The Living Christ as an exogenous agent? One sad evening many years ago a Scotsman asked Our Savior "What is Truth?". Today this ersatz Scot re-poses that question knowing that the answer transcends this realm.

If there were no Evil then could Good exist? Is Good an absolute or an epiphenomenon generated by its opposite?

Clerk Maxwell explained how Light must propagate through the void by the interaction of electricity with its complement magnetism. Our experience of the simple act of loving communion demonstrates that male and female must interact to propagate through time. Must Christ have his antithesis?

But in Matthew and Luke Jesus explains to us that the kingdom divided against itself cannot stand. Does this spell Desolation or Perpetual Propagation?

Some Delightful Things

24 October 1997

This afternoon the sky is blue and iced with powder like a delicious confection spangled with castor sugar. Flocks of clouds migrate and graze appearing with the cooling evening like creatures too well clothed for the height of noon. Against these shades of gray or white the wheeling flights of pigeons wear and whirry in shoals of silent splendor, gamboling in gratitude for their awaited sunshine.

As the sporting squadrons turn the uniform aspect of their wings beats the setting sun into coruscating glints of fulgent white. Then a swerve and tilt occults them to the gray invisibility of their backdrop. Another sweep another revolution and their shimmering shower dives again.

Finer than the magnesium bursts of our barbarous Autumn rituals are these, who proclaim their life before the infinity of the darkening skies, for they thank for life in their own way, scorning to gloat upon death.

In the gloaming of a Winter afternoon years ago an undergraduate mixed silver nitrate with ammoniacal liquor in Sonia Dunstan's laboratory and precipitated a storm of shimmering silver snow which billowed and convected around his test tube intestinally kneading itself like some meiotic cell about to engender a new sentience. Try as he might the experiment was unrepeatable. Was it that the pH was not quite right, the concentrations, the temperature? What trace catalysts were lacking, what surface effects, what unknown and adventitious preconditions of chemistry?

And yet the circling pigeons and the swirling silver are evanescent things the artefacts of circumstance metaphors of the greater Reality of which they are a part, unique and yet replicable.

One of the strangest metaphors I have read is in the paean to Charity of First Corinthians Thirteen. Much of Paul is dourly hortative and rather odd so that one wonders whether Thirteen is a plagiarism or an interpolation, so scintillating is its brilliance. As the author finishes his tender and powerful encomium upon the virtue of love he makes an assertion as startling and as anachronistic as it is famous: "For now we see through a glass, darkly;".

To us, familiar with glass and optical prosthetics of all kinds this may seem less than an original simile. But to the Romans, without telescopes, microscopes, cameras and only with windowpanes and tableware in the precincts of the rich this must have seemed well nigh incomprehensible. Why such a wrought metaphor, appealing it seems to a knowledge of technologies yet unborn?

Some would say that the ancients knew of these things because they were befriended by extraterrestrial animals who have since forsaken us. Some would say that this is the revealed Light of Christ who anticipates all things since He comprehends the track of time. Some shrug it off as one of those things, appealing to the proverbial troop of monkeys who given sufficient time replicate The Bard's ouvrage on a typewriter.

Perhaps the school of pigeons teaches us that things which are there may remain invisible. They may forever stay invisible lost against the incanous background of the infinite. Then they may turn, so without adjustment of their magnitude or range, they become apparent or even obvious. Maybe as our apposition to The Light modifies we discern where we once gazed in ignorance.

The glinting shower of silver flakes was latent in the clear and colorless fluid of my tube. It awaited only the conjunction of forces which would congeal. A different balance of influences would have born a jet-black colloid of minute motes of this brightest metal: Or a veiling mirror upon the glass which would have reflected my own face. Indeed "For now we see through a glass, darkly; but then face to face: now I know in part; but then shall I know even as also I am known".

What is Justice?

7 November 1997

Sometimes the radical feminists quip that history is "his story" and that justice is "just ice". It is good that some of their number have a sense of humor. And yet like all the most enduring jokes these disturb us with their kernels of truth.

When I was in Rome many things made a lasting impression upon me. Perhaps we know a nation by what it calls its secretariats. One thing I remember is that the Italians did not call their Home Office "The Ministry of Justice": They called it "The Ministry of Justice and Mercy". I hope and believe that it dispensed more of the latter!

Perhaps the Pagan ancients whose decaying monuments I had travelled to admire would have thought this appellation quaint, perhaps a little maudlin. For they took great pride in their history and great pride in their justice. They also knew much about vengeance, its exactment and its celebration in story. They did not, however, seem sensitive to the idea that History might be the chronicle of Pride, of Pride Deified, of Pride Reified in bloody deeds of Anger, Pride's pettish brat of a child. Neither, I am persuaded, did they discern that Justice is the License of Vengeance, the cold-eyed daughter of Judgment; or that Judgment issues of Pride as Man places himself in The Seat of God.

Society defines Crime. One learns much of a nation when one learns what it calls crime and what it does with, or to, the perpetrators. In my country, reserve understatement and lack of imagination are great social accomplishments. We used to kill malefactors by putting a rope round their necks and making the floor fall beneath them: A banal ritual, but final. Today we are much more enlightened. Serious crime is punished with twenty or thirty years of close incarceration offering splendid opportunities for education: Lifers have ample occasion to teach apprentices all the arts of iniquity. At the end of this stretch we have the satisfaction of knowing that the Victim is satisfied that the Malefactor is truly, tearfully sorry for his offence, that he is genuinely repentant and ardently desirous of a good and righteous future, that he has begged forgiveness of Christ and the Victim: The Perpetrator leaves the prison a good and useful man, kindly, honest and replete of knowledge, ready more than to repay in whatever days remain: Thirdly, Society is satisfied because a useless individual has been removed from the ambit of The Social Services where he would have been a dangerous drone and a drain upon the resources of the State.

This is Justice. A law is vindicated, a right is wronged, and all parties leave the precincts satisfied.

Once again patriotic Britons can look with justifiable pride to their lusty son, The Commonwealth of Massachusetts, where, in days gone by, they used to hang Quakers as well as less dangerous criminals. Americans are justifiably proud of their technical achievements. The more advanced states burn people to death with an electric current; inject them with synthetic venom or whatever but thankfully our Yankee cousins spurn such vulgarities relying with us upon the tried and true. If we had forgotten this then the recent affair of Louise Woodward, sentenced to fifteen years in a penitentiary (this is an American term though rather puzzlingly the Massachusetts authorities call their prison a "Corrections Institution") for the murder of an eight-month-old boy.

The killing of a baby is a vile act. Louise is indubitably a vile young woman, complicit in murder if not its direct agent. Or did I mistake her nonchalance for callousness and her innocent smiles for arrogance? Perhaps her contempt for her accusers won her fifteen instead of three years. If so, has justice been served or has vengeance?

What useful purpose is served by locking a woman into the company of sadists, lesbians and junkies? What useful purpose is served by assembling sadists, lesbians and junkies the more thoroughly to corrupt and be corrupted? Why do we agonise over a nineteen-year-old murderess in an American jail but not the drug courier in a Thai one, or indeed the Poll Tax evader in Winson Green?

The destruction of life may be just, but it is not equitable, never merciful and cheats Christ of a potential penitent.

I heard it said that by the time Louise left prison she would be beyond her child-bearing years. Whatever the biological plausibility of that remark it rather overlooks that Louise is in any case demonstrably unfit to nurture children.

What if anything should be done about this?

Nothing can restore Matthew to his Parents' arms. He is safely in those of Christ. Perhaps only Time and further issue can console them if they have little faith in their God. Perhaps the guilt of complicity or neglect, real or imagined, will haunt them. Most assuredly their friends should offer material and moral support in their time of grief, and The State should reinforce their efforts where it might. They have said that what they want is an admission of guilt, and it seems that contrition would give them as much satisfaction as a long sentence. Louise herself needs to confront her role in Matthew's death for the sake of her own well-being. She needs to weep for him and for her own wickedness, to adjust her attitudes to those weaker than herself and develop the responses that will make her a mother and a woman. Whatever her spiritual views that would be psychologically healthy. The State needs to abridge the public expense occasioned and to gain a good and useful citizen with all expedition, whilst deterring imitators and discharging its duty of ostensive governance.

Is there any gain to incarcerating a man for more than ten years or a teenager for more than three? Should prisoners be given taxing but useful work according to their abilities? Should they be allowed to take a legitimate pride in their achievements and re-establish their self-esteem?

If I am to be a follower of Christ I too must adjust my attitudes and responses. I must believe the unbelievable, think the unthinkable, mention the unmentionable and, in attaining the impossible, love the unlovable.

Louise should go to prison for three years only but for murder called murder. She should be guarded and visited by godly people and encouraged with prayers and kindness to confess her guilt, if to Christ and herself only. She should be given a light and unscarring whipping to sensitise her to fear and pain and instil a sympathy for those on the receiving end. She should otherwise be treated with gentleness and respect and given plenty of interesting work including supervised child care. At the end of her sentence she should be congratulated with a small party and a gift. And the British should pay for all this, since the problem is the natural consequence of their social attitudes and their regard for youth.

Some readers think I am a cruel and atavistic bigot who wishes to return to some mythic age of social indoctrination. Some of you think I am a ludicrous Quaker liberal, typical of what has caused the social malaise today. I ask both camps to consider the alternatives: Or is it one single option. The status quo. The symbiosis the Romans knew so well. The co-existence of spite, depravity and individual cruelty with the oppression, cynicism and collective rapacity of the state apparat?

I shall not ask for Justice, for I know that to obtain Justice is to encompass my destruction. This time is a time of Suffering but, like all Times, it is also a time of Reconstruction. I shall ask for Mercy, of God and of my Fellows, and hope to obtain Life.

Postscript: 12 June 2022

This is all very well, I suppose, but I am not sure, with a further twenty-five years of hindsight, that I had the formula right.

I have become less willing to write at length about social or political matters for I am less confident of my rectitude, and am sure that words are often wasted.

Rightly or wrongly, I am more certain of the essential presence of Evil in the human spirit, and that the dessert of all is damnation.

Therefore, if we desire Justice according to our deserving, then we should apply to Satan. If we desire Mercy, then we must apply to God.

At seventy, I am more confident than ever that supposedly supernatural agencies exist autonomous of the physical world and that they are the arbiters of Love, Good and Evil. Some of these agencies are interested in the welfare of humans, but for why I have no idea.

For sure, we may continue to seek vengeance, or merely the pragmatic deterrence of wicked acts, and I accept that the survival of civilization depends upon our continued vigilance. Notwithstanding, Justice is inaccessible to men: We are simply too transient, and too stupid, and too wicked.

CHAPTER FOUR

Out and Beyond

Jobs, Peace, Freedom

15 November 1997

Et in Arcadia Ego
Nicolas Poussin

      In the sunlit crepuscule of Europe's glades and arbors the ill-clad shepherds and well-fed shepherdesses reconvene their classic speculations. In a thousand pages and an hundred canvases the poets and the painters revisit the Elysian pastures of a time beyond time. Theirs is a world of order and content framed in the lineaments of a Pythagorean recession of perspective and proportion, rational yet humane.

      One of my own favorites is Nicolas Poussin[1], whose vision syncretises the Classical and the Christian, the Form and the Substance, the Mundane and the Ideal. The Louvre Museum retains a famous canvas that he painted in 1638-39 (The 2022 Wikipedia article says 1658). Much has been written of the complex geometric subframes of this and other Old Masters, perhaps not so much as of the complex pentagrams which haunt this picture's structure. Strange tales and stranger books abound about the painting's secret and hermetic meanings, its occult portents, and its coded paths to relics and to treasure. Half-hidden in the darkling mountain landscape of somber crags and forlorn peaks rests a fine plain ashlar tomb at which three strong and youthful shepherds pause and pose with natural ostentation. A sleek but statuesquely muscled woman rests her hand on a man regarding graven Roman words to which her fellow walkers point. The shepherds' forearms frame the edges of a regular pentagon, central yet rotated out of true. With stark angularity their fingers join the linear vortex that converges to the focal epitaph. The conclusion is mathematical: Inescapable, Inevitable and Self-defining:- *Et in Arcadia Ego*.

The trees of the subfusc alpine gloaming show their Autumn auburns beneath the vespertinal blues and golds of the etiolating sky. The baleful Pagan words cut deep last long but not forever even in stone.

Who or what is in the tomb? This is the stuff of speculation.

Few would identify Euston Square with Arcady. And yet a fine and colonnaded ashlar house sits there in neoclassical splendor, white with close-laid Portland facings like a cenotaph of faith.

The shepherds in the Poussin clearly each have jobs, their peace amidst the cool and mist-laced mountains reflects the liberty of their rangy calling.

But what do they do in the fine house on Euston Road? What do they shepherd and why? Where range they to extend the flocks of peace, the feet of freedom?

Now I read that yet more men and women are to be dismissed to defray a shortfall of some £600000, whilst in the same article its says that the house will be refurbished for £3.5 million in the same time scale.

The implications are mathematical.

There are some sixty thousand British Quakers. A man can live in London for some £30000 per annum. If each Quaker contributed £5 once to an employment subsidy then ten families could be supported for one more year. Quakers love Peace, and rightly for Christ enjoins it, and Quakers love Christ. But unemployment brings a form of death into life. It destroys the individual's self-esteem and confidence in his own capabilities and makes it virtually impossible to resume the career he trained for and is best at. He loses his ability to pay his way and his mortgage and his family loses its house whether it is faced with Portland stone or not. Dismissal leads to Destitution, Destitution to Despair, Despair to Desperation, Desperation to Destruction and Destruction to Death. The conclusion is Inevitable, Ineluctable, Self-fulfilling.

The same article continued. The £3.5m refurbishment fund had been subscribed by Friends and sympathisers as a set of interest-free loans, equivalent undiscounted to a £58.34 levy on each Quaker. What does Christ say of that? In Luke 7:30 He counsels "Give to every man that asketh of thee; and of him that taketh away thy goods ask them not again".

References

1. Public Domain Photograph of
"Et in Arcadia Ego" (Deuxième Version : 1628)
(Nicolas Poussin (1594 - 1665)
Louvre Museum Room 828
Taken from:-

   Wikipedia contributors. (2022, March 25).
   Et in Arcadia ego.
   In Wikipedia, The Free Encyclopedia.
   Retrieved 14:54, June 14, 2022, from
   https://en.wikipedia.org/w/index.php?title=Et_in_Arcadia_ego&oldid=1079126770

   Referred by:-
   Erwin Jurschitza ejurschi at directmedia.de
   Mo Apr 25 18:04:57 UTC 2005

The Ambiguous World of Alexander Ivanov

8 December 1997

<u>The Conceptions of the Painters</u>

     Though sometimes I like to try, I cannot choose the words to describe the sublimest visions of Men nor measure the devotion that moved their brush.

     As with the presentations of the natural world, I watch and wonder. Occasionally, I thought I apprehended their visions' meanings only to have my conceptions dashed as the ghost of understanding sidled from my mind, like directions garnered in a foreign bus station.

     Through two thousand years of Christian art, from the earliest hidden shepherds of the Catacombs, men and women have endeavored to display depths that the voice cannot explain. No pagan striving for divine emulations was affected: Only observant contemplation of the unseen imaginable.

     Certain things shine through sacred pictures, brought to life by the conscious and subconscious yearnings of a thousand great artists.

     In an Antiquity busy with heroes and colossi a Man of Sorrows extends the Compassion of the true God to the weak, the oppressed and the rejected: The woman, the cripple, the infected, the gay man and the exposed babe.

     Our race did not discover love or mercy, but somewhere beside the Rivers of Babylon the Jews of old discovered that quenchless quest for true Liberty that is the unique Judeo-European patrimony. The Greek and the Roman enjoyed the shadowed license of the rich but every civil thing we value today, our technical conveniences, our security of body and even the heritability of property devolves from the demotic Freedoms brought to Rome by Christ.

     In the Tretyakov Gallery in Moscow hangs a remarkable canvas by the Russian Nazarene painter Alexander Ivanov[1]. I am told that the word "Ivanov" translates as "Johnson": Whatever, this particular Son of Grace offers a vision disturbing in its blatancy and in its refinement.

     As Alexander painted much changed in his motherland. Another Alexander fought the Turk, defended Crimea and freed the serfs. Ivanov's picture is also about the passing of old orders and the transition to liberty. But Ivanov rejected the planar conventions of Oriental iconography, preferring the deep and geometrical chiaroscuros of Rome and her peerless tradition of votive imagery.

The canvas shows much which is distasteful to modern Anglo-American manhood. The male nudity, the epicene gestures, the neurasthenic fingers training long locks. The leering crouching figures are distressingly redolent of those nasty anti-Semitic lithographs which disfigured our streets in the latter half of Ivanov's century and the first of ours. The absence of women does nothing to reassure an embarrassed Briton who can surely sympathise with the generations of well-bred Muscovites who pretended not to notice as they hustled their families past this active and arresting landscape on many a wet museum afternoon!

But if we suspend the judgments of our time and race we enter a scene where surprise, expectancy and hesitation converge in the delight of purest love.

The Sun is setting in vapored autumnal splendor behind the atramental shades of hulking rugged peaks. Across a distant lake a luminous mist extends a striking demarkation above a great and sprawling city where masts crowd the distant harbor and yet no lamps greet the dusktide landfall. Before these remote and distant ranges rests an high and arid outcrop lit with the sun of evening and relieved by a deep and tranquil river with stunted but leafy verdure on the painting's left-hand margin. Across the foreground and the right side curves a crowd of cloth-draped tribesmen.

On the extreme right-hand two ill-clad and iron-helmed horsemen whose fine steeds belie their riders turn their heads in bemused query as they bridle back their mounts. Who are these strong but rudely caparisoned soldiers? Are they auxiliaries in the pay of Antipas come to investigate a seditious assembly? Before these, wool-wound and turbaned elders bring their gray beards to a bathing at the mossy sandstone bankside of a sacred stream. On the extreme left-hand a bald and sinewed figure rests his weight upon his staff as standing still in water he regards the nascent tumult. Beside him a naked youth springs with impudent impulse from the river but is beckoned by a girlish figure to restrain his careless rush.

"The Appearance of Christ to the People"
by Alexander Ivanov
1837-1857

      In the center startled sitters turn in expectation as a red and purple figure gazes into the canvas, helping a candid-gowned patriarch to rise to his feet. To the foreground right, shivering emergers catch the air of new-found promise as a pallid nude turns like a lurching olympian to the object of the stir. Near to the picture's center a gauntly hide-clad Baptist lifts his arms in hailing indication of a lone purposive approacher striding the golden rock beyond.

      The Figure of Christ is draped richly but plainly in a deep blue cloak and deep red coat. He is erect serene and composed. He is walking on rock and yet it seems, perhaps by a trick of perspective, that he is not truly of this dimension. He has not arrived and yet was ever here: Imminent yet Immanent. I do not know whether these homophones pun in Russian; but Russians sure know the distinction and the paradox. His distant Form cuts the horizon of glowing mist so far behind across the lake. And yet in a remarkable sense He seems to be at One with the nebulous distance from which He, too, emerges but which His Substance interrupts. His intended Path is at variance with that of the rest, and yet towards them.

The composition's focal geometry is very striking and I suspected the canvas of being constructed on Phidian principles. The Ratio of Phidias[2] is a transcendental mathematical constant (unity plus the square root of five, then halved). It has a range of interesting recursive properties in the generation of Fibonacci series and other mathematical forms and for many centuries Western artists have used it to divide pictures and modellings in the most visually-harmonious ways. It is thought to have been introduced in a primitive form by the great Periclean sculptor and architect Phidias, a key participant in the design of The Parthenon. All Poussin work and that of many other masters uses the ratio in compositional planning. But astonishingly this same number has been found to occur in the structural design of living organisms and their seeds. Few of us would now dare to offer, with Leibnitz, a mathematical Proof of God. But does this number, whose exact value can only be approached and never attained, betray The Hand of a Divine Creator, and if so is He an artist?

I investigated my geometrical suspicions with the appropriate analysis. The reproduction in my Phaidon is some 76.5 by 110.5 millimeters whilst the original is about 540 by 750 centimeters. Neither aspect ratio is Phidian ($\Phi \approx 1.618$) but the 4% discrepancy indicates that the picture in the book has tolerable similitude to the canvas. Since the glowing line of the horizon fog transects The Heart of Christ I identified That latter with the vanishing point and quartered the painting about it. But the horizontal and vertical ratios mapped proved respectively to be 2:1 and 2.2:1 not 1.618:1. We therefore infer simple quartering by thirds rather than the Classical scheme. The major perspective line crosses the bare youth's scalp, the girlish man's restraining hand, and The Baptist's right hand index finger before converging on The Heart of Christ. A shorter line orthogonal to it passes through the spine of the twisting "Olympian" nude. Both these lines also converge on The Heart and are clearly rotated with respect to the quartering orthogonals. I speculated that there might be a Trinitarian significance to the angle of rotation. Maybe it was 30° ($\pi/6$ radians). Tracing paper and a school protractor quickly disabused me of this second error: It is 20° ($\pi/9$ radians). Nine is of course the square of three, but never one for numerology I am reluctant to read arcane but tenuous hermeneutics into such artifacts.

Clearly I am untrained competently to delineate the sacred iconography of a devotional canvas so I ask you, Who is the moping dreamer in unregarding prayer above the river bank? Who the wildly-visaged Petrine atavus beneath the straggling bankside boughs. The figure whose blue and red raiment echoes those of Christ above, that one who assists the shrouded patriarch to his feet:- Does he prefigure Him who raised Lazarus?

I started this description with the lay of land and light. Let us look again. The Sun is setting behind the far mountains. And yet, notwithstanding the Levantine latitude, it is frontlighting with auric warmth the bathers before our gaze. The Jordan is a deep and tranquil pool which must tumble in a truly Roraiman cataract meters behind the tree for we must be a good two hundred above the city of the plain. So if we are East of Galilee the distant high sierra bears no resemblance to the

Explanatory Illustration for the Analysis of "The Appearance of Christ to the People"

scree-skirted arenitic tablelands around The Horns of Hattin. But, should you object, we are looking toward a dawn then where are the softly arid billows of the Hills of Golan? Where does Christ stand in this strange dilemma? His Shadow throws top right indicating a light source which frontlights the people.

Is it too fantastic to think that Christ really is Coming with a Message, a Message which Ivanov is relaying with devout hands? A Message full of paradox, wholly simple yet inscrutably complex? A Message which transcends the time of geology, the space of solar evolutions and the spilling search of waters? A Message which contradicts our pet assumptions, turns logic on its head and sets our sums at naught?

Bibliography

1. "The Art Book"
   No Listed Author   1994
   Phaidon Press Limited of London
   ISBN 0-7148-3625-7
   (This book is available in a larger format)

2. "The Divine Proportion"
   "A Study in Mathematical Beauty"
   H E Huntly   1970
   Dover Publications Incorporated of New York
   ISBN 0-486-22254-3

   Jim Warren discussed:-
   "The Appearance of Christ to the People"
   Oil on Canvas
   Painted 1837-1857
   by
   Alexander Ivanov (1806-1858)
   The Tretyakov Gallery, Moscow

Problems that Remain

20 December 1997

Geoffrey Hubbard is an experienced scientist and gifted writer who came to Christ in maturity and went on to become a "Quaker by Convincement"[1]. His fact-filled synopsis of The Society of Friends in Britain flounders in its middle passages where he confronts a description of God, for what can any of us write of something discerned but not descried, glimpsed fleetingly through the smoke of human commotion, something shy of summons and of all instrumentalities?

Why have I plagiarised another man's chapter heading? Because I cannot improve upon it. And yet I wonder if a Problem of the mind is not an Opportunity of the spirit.

Hubbard's chapter introduces Quakerism as the dogma-free religion stripped of ritual. But by rejecting dogma do we not decide a doctrine? I am reminded of the kindly Friend who set his devout ideas on paper and honored this stranger with their gift. After pages extolling God and Peace he interpolated Total Abstinence: Setting those words in capitals and underlining them twice. Totality cannot be made more total by rubrication, but what is more dogmatic than totality?

Hubbard's three salient problems may be summarised as:-

(a) The Problem of Purpose
(b) The Problem of Omnipotence
(c) The Problem of Immanence

All three of these concepts interpenetrate but to manage my discussion I shall attempt a separation.

<u>The Problem of Purpose</u>

Our Western culture is incorrigibly and perhaps now irrevocably etiological. For every effect we assign a cause and none rest till that precursor is identified. But this only postpones the evil hour at which we must quest again, for the Primal Agent recedes like a figure in opposed mirrors and must be hunted anew.

But what is the Cause and what the Effect? Birds gambol in the sunlight. What causes the gamboling? Does the sunlight cause the birds to gambol? Do the birds cause the gamboling? Does sunlight cause birds?

When I was a doctoral student I was asked "what causes rivers to meander?". Some point to Substance: "It is sand". Some to Form: "It is slope". The geologist says: "It is alternating skew-shoals", the physicist: "It is vortices". I said it had something to do with the Fourier Series of ptygmatic wave forms and I programmed computers to prove it. My supervisor, the late Professor DIH Barr, complained "Mr Warren, you are one of those hydraulicians whose whole treatise can be read without the reader ever once learning that water is wet". Of course he was right. The answer is "water".

Two cosmological models remain. The Hubblian postulate says that the universe exploded from an infinitely dense mote of infinitely energetic primal matter. We tell ourselves that we can relate the history of the burst's first nanoseconds. But why did this speck of potential form, and why in that place and time? The Hoylian postulate, now "discredited", says that matter wells from sources into a continuum which presumably cycles back to whence it came. (I oversimplify of course). But why does it do that and what did it do before it essayed such adventures?

Etiology is at the hearts of science and religion but what can finite men know of The Infinitely Remote? For when we exorcise those sirens at our flanks, Past and Future, we are left with the naked now of known sensation. All else is speculation.

Men believe in the future. They plan. Their purpose is their act of faith. Why project Purpose upon That which will not perish and has no Plan? We hear much of "planned parenthood". But do even mere creatures need to plan their issue to love it? If we can love the fruit of happenstance, why will we not allow God that privilege?

The Problem of Omnipotence

Does evil exist and if so in what does it consist? Did God create Evil when he rejected Lucifer? If God is good and all-powerful why does he tolerate evil? If God is Pure Love then why has He created creatures who suffer, hate and die in pain? Do we create evil when we reject? What is the nature of power in all its diverse manifestations?

If earthly life is in the nature of a test or examination of candidates, then why try men whose true characters are instantly transparent? If

God is love and an all-powerful father then why the gift of Free Will so that we may live eternally or die eternally of our volitions? For Christ said (Matthew 7:9;11) "Or what man is there of you, whom if his son ask bread, will he give him a stone? Or if he ask a fish, will he give him a serpent? If ye then, being evil, know how to give good gifts unto your children, how much more shall your Father which is in heaven give good things to them that ask him?"

An earthly father is empowered to grant or withhold earthly things. We do not know the character or extent of Divine empowerment but experience suggests that it is not exercised upon mundane needs. And our logic suggests, weak and silly though it is, that Free Will is not consistent with Divine Omnipotence. Does it make better sense to see God truly as Father: As Loving and Powerful, but also vulnerable and far from infallible? Only the fallible can repent and Our Divine Father repented when he beheld the Error of His Children and sent Christ to Deliver them. There is a very intimate connection between power, rejection and evil but it is very difficult for men and women to trace the nexus.

If God is good perhaps He is more interested in affinity than potency. If The Society of Friends follows a similar paradigm maybe much of its longevity in the face of sparsity is explained.

Much of power is used to fetch, garner and create. But if God is not a creator in the creaturely way we understand, then power as we know it is redundant. Power as we know it is very physical. Physicists tell us that it is the dividend of energy and time. But in a Realm where matter (energy) is null and time has no meaning, the Dwelling-place of the Eternal Spirit, what relevancy has power? Rockets cannot take men to that Realm for it exists in the late Carl Sagan's "spaceship of the imagination" though perhaps not there only.

Matthew 14:15;21 relates The Feeding of the Five Thousand with the five loaves and the two fishes. They are hard, hard words for he who respects The Laws of Conservation and they were doubtless a stumblingblock to Hubbard as to me. But is Christ doling matter or breaking time? Perhaps what He is really giving is Love, which doubles and re-trebles on every shared division.

<u>The Problem of Immanence</u>

Is God ubiquitous and if so how pervasive? Is it meaningful to visualise God as an ethereal and coextensive influence like a vast faradic flux field soaking the Universe with a sentient presence? The ancients speak much of The Light and I suppose light is still the most accessible approximation of ubiquity. What is the relationship (if any) between Immanence and The (

Quaker) Light Within? Can this presence justify The Friends' witness to "that of God in every man"?

What does this mean?

When I first went to a Quaker Meeting House I was not sure where it was. I found it in the center of a large and modern city, sequestered, or perhaps concealed, between forbidding office blocks. It was only twenty minutes to the advertised time of worship but the black iron gates of its narrow ginnel, wrought it seemed to defend Sedan, were resolutely shut and the drear yard beyond lifeless. I idled some more time walking beside the luminous cathedral two streets away, watching the pigeons, the hurrying votaries and inspecting the funeral flowers for a dead princess. I was very frightened. I wanted to walk back to my car and drive home. Quakers were strange. Powerful yet pacific, remote, exclusive, Christian yet compassionate. Would they welcome me? Would they ask me to go away and apply for membership? Would they be all over their new proselyte? Would I just coldly be ignored? Interviewed? Interrogated? Suddenly, beside the pigeons, I felt an ineluctable force as if an enormous electromagnet had grasped every iron atom in every ligand of my blood and was towing me relentlessly to the House. When I reached the doors two elderly people asked me who I was and which Meeting I had come from. I tremblingly confessed I was no Member and had never been before but they were gentle and friendly.

A few months earlier I had been alone in a confrontation at work. I was surrounded by enemies. I was tense but not afraid. People started swearing at me and physical violence seemed inevitable. Yet a strange and balmy feeling came over me that although I was helpless my enemies were *completely helpless* and I felt a weird serene comfort. The swearing and the menace stopped. I believe Christ rescued me that day.

This thing is, like the love for a woman, impossible to explain and cannot convince those who have not experienced it of its own objective existence. For them it can only be sentimentality or cant. It has nothing to do with hormones, Dopamine or other opiates. I know what it means to be drugged and it is wholly dissimilar. It is something as different as difference can be to the concept of The God of the Interstices which brings no honor to God and less to men, a concept which ludicrously patronises God, relegating Him to shrinking domains as yet unexplained by the wisdom of man. That is base and mindless superstition, anthropocentric, different again to the reverent and principled rejection of Deity whether on intellectual or ethical grounds.

Men do not comprehend God. Power and Action and Influence are differently understood by The Creator and the created.

God is everywhere or nowhere. He is with us in our dangers and our ecstasies, in the spreading splendor of the firmament and the delicacy of the twinkling stars. In the fury of the breaking waves and the phosphorescent combs of tiny creatures. He is in the suffering and the reconstruction and whatever it means to transit from Death to Life He is there.

Bibliography

1	"Quaker by Convincement"	
	Geoffrey Hubbard	1985
	The Quaker Home Service of London	
	ISBN 0-85245-189-X	

Bunhill Fields

11-12 January 1998

For some weeks I have projected a new adventure and cannot tell if I have yet completed it. I do not know whether it is a pilgrimage, a homage or an excuse for a pub crawl that somehow went badly wrong. I wished to meet a man I thought I understood, to commune in silence and take my leave fulfilledly.

Some months ago I read one of those Christian writers who said that the *genius loci* was the archetypal heathen deity; that Satan was a lord of places whose earth-bound minions jealously guarded their Appointed plots; but that the Power of Christ confounded these terminunculi and voided the tyranny of Place. He went on to illustrate the principle with an anecdote about a defensive steward-like worker he had encountered when he had entered a premises, presumably upon a pastoral mission. The author said that a few minutes of inward prayer disarmed this satanic pylorus who presently became quite accommodating. I find this story wholly credible. I have frequently encountered sinful if not satanic stewards on my rounds, though inevitably through my prideful habit of gazing into lavatory mirrors.

Before I turned to Christ I could feel the melancholic electricity of The Place, its raiment of mist and sunlight its innate character and texture. Some places were restful, some wistful, several sordid and a few unnerving. I wrote several poems most of which were named for places and all of which were strongly located. My interests and my scientific training gave primacy to place and with place I felt secure and to place I would always home. Since my conversion places have somehow lost much of their charm as I commune with a Spirit who is everywhere and everywhen, yet absent from mundane dimensions.

So perhaps you feel something of my foreboding, my hesitancy, and my caution as I stalk with trepidation but with tempted steps of longing to a chartered bounded precinct, and that a graveyard?

Maybe fifteen months ago I found in Foyle's a tidy stand of well-cased literary classics uniformly produced by the same publisher. A volume called "Poems and Prophecies"[1] of William Blake caught my eye but I did not buy it as I was a bit strapped. I did, however, remember the price: £9.99. On the Tuesday before Christmas last year I returned to London with a few more funds and sought again the tidy bookstand. It was nowhere to be found for in the intervening twelve month Foyle's had reverted to its traditional disarray and it appeared that only odd copies of that publisher's volumes were scattered about. A few minutes search, however, located the main display on new shelves elsewhere. But now new temptation and new perplexity obtruded. A notice said that two volumes for the price of one could be had upon "selected" titles. Would such "selection" include the Blake? If so what should I purchase with the Blake? Milton? Homer? Virgil? What if I would be asked to pay full price for the Blake only or the same money for two other tomes?

I selected the Blake and the Milton[2] copies and reminded the clerk of the "two for one" offer. He accepted £9.99 for both books without demurral and yet I felt embarrassed and disquieted. For the clerk did not make it clear to me whether I was getting the Blake for free or the Milton. You see, Milton is a genius but Blake merely an eccentric and whilst priceless genius should be gratis to all good students mere eccentricity is not worth paying for. I thought about complaining to the young man but he may have misapprehended the nature of my problem.

Why is Milton a genius but Blake an eccentric? The answer to this question has to do with both society and fashion. The son of a City notary, John Milton was born in 1608 and educated at St Paul's School and Christ's College, Cambridge. Clearly he was in youth a member of The Established Church. You see, John Milton was a comfortable middle-class polemicist, versed early in the Ancient authors, and his prime years of Puritan life caught the cusp of Cromwell's Commonwealth. But he was no canting opportunist, instead a tortured devotee, perplexed by the nature of temptation and the Benisons of God. A learned man who bore his letters lightly he nevertheless invokes "divinest Melancoly" through measured sentences of breathless gravity. Blake his Georgian acolyte was born in 1757 and came to maturity in The Napoleonic Era. William Blake was the son of a Soho hosier who schooled as an engraver and earned his living as a commercial artist. Blake was working-class and his time was sold to others leaving his life's work in the margins of his days. But for all his professed contempt for education Blake was no ignoramus and loved the Hebrew and Pagan classics from an early age. Blake was a mystic visionary in an age of reason. Painter, poet, prophet, his etchings and engravings fly with wind-tossed fury as men, beasts and angels strain starkly sinewed limnings across the vaults of heaven or skulk with fear-drawn faces within their freezing tombs of fusain. An Elysian romantic whose poems bubble brook-like with enthusiastic chatter: Not as a child or much less a madman but like an amateur over-enthralled with his hobby.

Blake's major weakness was to reject a dialog with his time. And yet this lends him a certain celestial timelessness, a negation of time and place, or rather the transcendence lent by the Spiritual. In the age of Laplace, Blake hated the memory of Newton whose infinitesimal evolutions set the solar clockwork ticking. Yet, unlike Dante, Blake could advance no competing cosmology with which to convince a skeptical public.

It would never have occurred to Milton defensively to rail against science. He would have considered science an obscure and dilettante pastime, useful chiefly for embarrassing the papacy. It is worth remembering that even by Blake's day many scientists were ordained men who saw their work as Praise of God by better manifesting His Design to a benighted World. Acceptance of the Axioms of Euclid (or Riemann or Lobachevsky) or the unvarnished impressions of experience is always a Vote of Faith. Thus science has much of the fiduciary character of classical religion. Because, however, it is Praise without Prayer it is dangerously value-free and perhaps that is what appalled the printer prophet as his genius was impressed between the forme of Authority and the platen of Conviction. So science is a reversion to classical Paganism in its worship of nature but differs from that in its conception of the disinterested Godhead and therefore sat snugly with both the deism and the atheism of The Enlightenment. Those who see Blake as an incondite extension of Gray's Romantic prospectus can credibly point to The Book of Thel (1789) a tender and touching, but unsentimental, allegory. Certainly Linnaeus, de Saussure, Lamarke and William Smith would have had no difficulties with this very earthly vision of organic and atmospheric metaphors, though at that time a distinction was imagined to exist between the vital and physical sciences.

Today we find it difficult to interpret the following words as anything other than a (meta)physical postulate:-

> Without Contraries is no progression. Attraction
> and Repulsion, Reason and Energy, Love and Hate,
> are necessary to Human Existence.[a]

Yet Blake saw no inconsistency between that and the apparently static, dismissive vision implied by:-

> The Atoms of Democritus
> And Newton's Particles of Light
> Are sands upon the Red sea shore
> Where Israel's tents do shine so bright.[b]

Duration is at the heart of the scientific interpretation of existence. The lofty Milton has this to say "On Time":-

> And Joy shall overtake us as a flood;
> When every thing that is sincerely good,
> And perfectly divine,
> With Truth, and Peace, and Love, shall ever shine[c]

because like his successor Addison he inhabits an integrated universe where the natural world is godly but subject and shall be superseded when the Appointed Day arrives.

In contrast Blake's even more lovely words are wholly anthropo-referential and abstracted into an entirely moral realm where time and space are irrelevant:-

> And all must love the human form
> In heathen, turk or jew.
> Where Mercy Love & Pity dwell
> There God is dwelling too.[d]

It was with this last sentiment in mind that I retired for lunch before catching the tube to Old Street. It occurred to me that William Blake had been penalised, even in death, for his non-conforming views. It is very likely that he was a follower of Emanuel Swedenborg (1688-1772), a Swedish scientist and theologian who settled in London and there propounded Quaker-like ideas. Swedenborg contemplates an inner light of Divine Grace inherent in men and celebrated by the above verse. Like Quakers, Swedenborgians seem to have favored silent worship and to have avoided professional priesthoods. In any event, there is a marked anti-clericalism in Blake's writings though he tended to tone it down for publication as can readily be seen when the several variorums of "The Garden of Love" are traced. Whilst neither Quakerism or Swedenborgianism are actively anti-clerical they share with Blake the belief in God in Every Creature and it is likely that Blake adopted this concept from Swedenborg in early youth, perhaps after meeting the mystic in person. In many of Blake's Songs, including famously "The Tyger", this belief in the divine inspiration of the animal is strongly projected.

When I emerged at Old Street the gray still air of midwinter hung damply like a saturated garland across the soaked and spattered sidewalks of City Road. It was late lunchtime and the pullulating suits were striding three abreast to their dowdy postwar offices. This was ever the dog-eared end of The City's chartered compass, two hundred years ago a shunned ribbon of blighted ground separating the metalworking districts of Holborn and Clerkenwell from the Huguenot silk-lofts of Shoreditch and Spitalfields. The area had been intensively bombed in World War Two but no Polumbo or de Vries had seen fit to try his talents here. I ambled South past the shop that specialises in company flotations and The Seattle Coffee Company which serves a mean cappuccino. I wondered if in the former establishment they might make me a company to measure taking into account my girth and stature and the weather and whim of the season. Would such an enterprise float more like the creamy froth on the cappuccino or more like the discarded Embassy packet which graced the stagnant sump of the traffic-coned cable-trench? With a little care I found the gate to Bunhill Fields burial ground. The carved red granite gate posts read that the ground had first been made available for interments in 1665 as the plague gathered momentum and an isolated extramural site was required for the infected dead. As the plague subsided the unconsecrated plot was made over to bury the heretics unfit to profane the circumvallated City or share the rest of the faithful. I read with astonishment that before The Fields were closed in 1857, one hundred and sixty thousand persons were there inhumed.

Across The Fields lay Bunhill Row where Blake's cynosure the blind Milton wrote "Paradise Lost" as the epidemic grew and The Fields opened, for he too was an outcast in a Royalist land. It is difficult, however, to see as blind a man with Vision to write:-

> His words here ended; but his meek aspéct
> Silent yet spake, and breathed immortal love
> To mortal men,...[e]

I entered the graveyard. The guidebooks had told me of the many noble planes which shaded the meditative sitter from the Sun of Summer, but the only exfoliants I saw were the peeling flags of ponding Portland stone along the crossing walkways. Also I had read of the profusion of wild flowers which softened with gay delight the somber stones of this urban oasis. But the only wild flowers I found were these flowers of London town, the devout and dissident men and women who had graced a sullen country to here be discarded like withered wreaths of triumph. White crowded ranks of limestone headstones etched blank of all memorials by the acid rains of centuries infested every foot of ground. Black iron railings separated the living from the dead as lone walkers hurried through the massing graves. In a broad crossing I found the stone thought to be near to Blake's resting place, next to Defoe's obelisk. Blake's parents also lie somewhere here. I paused at the stone and offered a prayer of thanksgiving for the compassion and genius of William but I did not pray for him as I take his Everlasting Ecstasy for granted. Further across the graveyard I encountered by surprise the resting place of Thomas Bayes the statistician and said a similar prayer requesting just a tiny part of the goodness and the talent of these two fine men. Bayes presence puzzled me as I thought he was an Anglican vicar. Later reading discovered that Bayes was the Presbyterian minister at Tonbridge Wells where he died. His father had been the Presbyterian minister in Leather Lane (Clerkenwell) and the younger Bayes had been brought back to London for burial in the family plot. It is intriguing that even Presbyterians were buried as heretics since their church is that Established in Scotland. John Milton died a member of The Established Church and is buried intramurally 650 meters South-West of Bunhill Fields at St Giles, Cripplegate, now an ancient church isolated in the midst of the Barbican development.

I entered Bunhill Row and walked South through the invisible wall. Modest and understated stands a little black cast iron obelisk in the middle of Moor Lane. Picked out in white are cast reliefs: a vertical line with "CITY OF LONDON" on its Southern side. The young Japanese women patiently awaited their lifts as they stood on the granolithic steps of their polished plate glass banks. They almost certainly thought that the little pillar was just a traffic bollard decorated with the customer's name and would have been incredulous to learn that that on the Southern side was London and that on the Northern somewhere else.

A studious eye can still discern a subtle but abrupt change in wealth and function at that boundary but the living and expanding world of London has long embraced the ejected remnants of heathens, heretics, turks, jews and all. For though it is our habit to think of a great city as an aggrandising organism amoebically growing from its nucleus it is in reality the congregation of centripetal creatures who meet by migration to where their aspirations may be shared and fulfilled. The divisions and the doctrines of old have lost their import for the native and the immigrant alike. To today's denizens of City and city Bunhill Fields is an unregarded relic, another ancient graveyard keeping who knows who.

Last Sunday another migrant to another land spoke to me through a Friend from the days of Bunhill's prime. In the Doric prose and shining metaphor of Milton's century he said to me:-

The humble, meek, merciful, just, pious, and devout souls are everywhere of one religion; and when death has taken off the mask they will know one another, though the divers liveries they wear here makes them strangers.[3]

References

1. "Poems and Prophesies"
   William Blake
   (Edited by David Campbell)
   Everymans Library
   ISBN 1-85715-034-1
   1991

2. "The Complete English Poems"
   John Milton
   (Edited by Gordon Campbell)
   Everymans Library
   ISBN 1-85715-097-X
   1992

3. "Quaker Faith and Practice"
   The Yearly Meeting of
   The Religious Society of Friends in Britain
   ISBN 0-85245-269-1
   (Quotation from the writings of
     William Penn, 1693)
   1995

a. The Argument
   "The Marriage of Heaven and Hell"

b. "Mock on, Mock on!..."
   (Untitled Poem)
   Lines 9-12
   From The Rossetti Manuscript in The British Museum

c. "On Time"
   Lines 13-16

d. "The Divine Image"
   Lines 17-20

e   "Paradise Lost"
Book III
Lines 266-268

The Reprieve of War

21 February 1998

Language is a funny thing. Hardly rational it contains a jumbled heap of honed and crafted clichés cast into the dark absconded caverns of the mind like the dejected arms of a routed army, a sequestered trove of trusted weapons, secreted for a future skirmish.

One such old and tarnished forging comes to mind on this bright but dreary afternoon: "The Eve of War". How often have you read those words before? You have forgotten the many contexts and its original, perhaps anonymous, author. Yet how pregnant is this desolate phrase with the cool and calm crepuscule of *fin de siècle* nostalgia, the balm and surety of a sunlit ancient order helpless upon the track of destiny. How fulfilled yet waiting upon the ugly promise of pain and confusion, of futility and change, and an uncertain new beginning.

We look back to the Edwardian Era or the Thirties as melancholic Golden Ages of old courtesies, well-bred pleasures and stable standards underwriting a troubled plenty. Today I walked in King George Park and repaired to my accustomed bench where I often sat in Summer and thought of Christ. I prayed Him to help us avert the breaking conflict: To turn our minds from Pride and the nomism that masks our Lust of Vengeance. I looked across to the file of poplars whose glaucous leaves shimmered in the arid breeze of Summer and whose gaunt and gracile brushes now swept the cool wet winds of an early and unnatural Spring. As I sat the distant shouts of players subsided into stillness as the teams quit their field for the clubhouse showers behind me. The Captain retrieved his oval ball and walked past my seat where he asked of me the time. I said "two eighteen" and thanking me he left me to the parting clouds, the breaking sun, the cycling piping children and the gruffly sporting househounds. Now the sunstruck lawnlaid landscape with its distant leisured business took the hue of a Netherlandish Master as I crossed the flagflown touchline and walked the short straight alameda with its virid spherococcus flamed across the sunstoked tree trunks in the setting Winter sun.

The dawn of Monday morning brings reprieve. Through no virtue of the petty contenders a giant intercedes. We survive to sin again. The living death limps on. We bluster and hide our arms like boys surprised with dirty books. With smiling relief we untense and relax our guard as The Master approaches.

Woman and Child in
The Vision of Nicolas Poussin

21 February 1998

**"Moses Saved from the Bulrushes"
by Nicolas Poussin
1638**

How like the washed abundance of an Autumn dawn are the works of the great French Classical painter Nicolas Poussin[2] in their light and languor and yet how active in pose and purpose. After a pugnacious youth Poussin became a shy and uxorious man given to the meticulous development of his chosen themes and evasive of fashionable but fatuous commissions from the kings and courtiers of his time. But to this extent he was a man of his age: He knew The Bible and the Pagan Authors by heart and referred his vision and his temper to the precepts of the Ancients. To this extent he was a man not of his time: Women were important, as agents as well as victims, as the makers of history as well as the makers of men. Poussin was of course a Catholic and yet this aspect of his mind would have engaged the agreement of the fathers and mothers of Quakerism who were his contemporaries. For to this extent Poussin is a man for all times: He is a Stoic prophet of acceptance and rejection which cohere his every work.

"Moses Saved from the Bulrushes"[a] presents a boldly frontlit tableau of vibrant primary colors backed by deep but muted landscapes. Beneath the somber distant skies rests a soft but bleak escarpment at whose feet tumbles a dusty town. In the middle ground rests a wide and placid river whose bleary satin surface echos the blue above. Before the distant town strikes a bold arched ashlar bridge which is perfectly horizontal and with its denticulated parapets and pilastered chapel lends a very Roman balance to the pyramid at its end.

Full of purpose is this picture. From the far shore skulls a ferry with its saffron-coated crosser whilst nearby toga-clad students pause to study the stream. All these rearward adumbrations are diffusely brushed with subdued colors whilst the foreground tableau is boldly lit and tightly shadowed with sharply-limned edges and closely-modelled contours. Slightly left of center a large and princely woman rests her arm upon a handmaid and points with regal languor at a well-fed foundling babe. Wound in a gown of saffron bound with a ruby brooch of gold her blonde and braided coiffure betrays a woman whose toilet costs time if not money. To her left stands a noble Italian companion whose leanly handsome features bear a smile of refined surprise as she displays her palms in wonder at the retrieval from the flood. Behind these young and queenly beauties reclines a tanned and bearded power whose incanous laurelled head regards his fluvial realm. But regardless of his genius stand the three enamored ladies as their well-fed rich-clad slavegirl stoops to lift the chubby youngster from an oval wicker tray. Bearing the boy from the waters rises a tanned and frank man whose well-toned musculature occludes all sinew. Now Exodus 2:7 affirms that Moses's sister affected to share the princess'es surprise and suggest that she herself find a wet nurse: Is the "Italian" lady Poussin's idea of a Semitic sister? Exodus 2:5 avers that the princess'es maid fetched the child. It is Josephus who interposes the help of a male swimmer. Clad in the same murex blue as the delighted Roman lady, this swimmer is neither a starved mean slave nor is he a flabby eunuch. For this is a world of order but not of oppression. A world where the long ostensive finger of royal womanhood decrees charity and acceptance, where the clement hand of Love rescues The Giver of the Laws.

My Phaidon[1] declares this canvas to measure 85 by 121 centimeters and I have measured the picture in the book at 173 by 242 millimeters, yielding a ratio error of 1.8%. Accordingly the following geometrical assessments are tenable. Firstly, however, it should be said that all Poussin canvases are constructed upon Phidian principles where The (Greater) Ratio of Phidias has a numeric value near to 1.618. When Poussin intends to develop a narrative in terms of parallel perspectival planes he uses rectilinear constructional elements as in the famous Arcadian Shepherds[b] picture in the Louvre or in the present painting. When on the contrary he elects to integrate sight-lines *through* a picture he reverts to crossing curvilinear elements as in the two Plutarchian canvases "Landscape with the Body of Phocion Carried out of Athens, 1648"[c] and "Landscape with the Ashes of Phocion Collected by his Widow, 1648"[d], respectively in The National Museum of Wales and in The Walker. These remarks apply to the original canvas area displayed in the Phaidon illustration without the seventeenth-century extensions included in the Zwemmer[2].

The major perspectival line runs from the top left to the bottom right of the canvas crossing The Heart of Pharaoh's Daughter, and follows her extended forearm and index finger, then intersecting the mouth of the slavegirl and the mouth of Moses. The heart of Pharaoh's Daughter is the Phidian focus of this picture positioned both vertically and horizontally at $1:\varphi$. The tip of her straight nose, vertically above her heart is at a vertical ratio of $1:(1+\varphi)$. There is a subsidiary mathematical focus in the bottom right at the philtrum of the stooping slavegirl. This focus is, however, aspect-referential. Allow that h is the horizontal width of this rectangular canvas and that v is its height. Then the aspect ratio, $r=h/v$, of the canvas is 1.4235 and the horizontal displacement of the girl's face from the picture's left edge is v and its vertical displacement from the top edge is v/r. It is accordingly probable that Poussin intends to associate the rational apprehension of servile senses with the transcendental Will of the Heart in an inseparable linkage with the imperative gesture of Command and the Mouth that shall lead Israel to The Laws. The river god at bottom left balances the Pagan monument at top right whilst the bridge chapel at top left is a foil to Moses bottom right.

Women are on top and smile with firm command to accept the human flotsam discarded by his own.

I turn now to a very different painting with a much more saturnine tone. It is, however, by the same master and presents the same prospectus. It is called "Christ and the Woman taken in Adultery, 1653"[e].

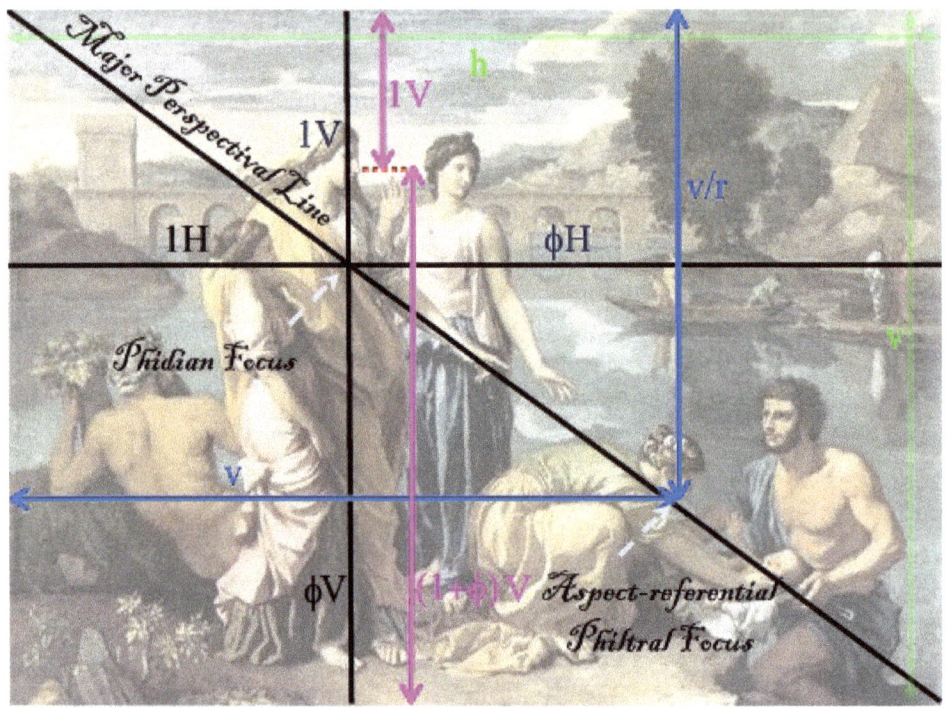

**Explanatory Illustration for the
Analysis of "Moses Saved from the Bulrushes"**

**"Christ and the Woman Taken in Adultery"
by Nicolas Poussin
1653**

      A desolate streetscape of monumental edifices austere behind arched and pilastered curtain walls looms with a limonitic bloom beneath a cerulean sky fleeced with vespertinal cumuli. The enormous ashlar blocks and the ramping central balustrade impress with a geometric megalomania which two tiny figures, a flower-planted vase and a vestal smudge of smoke accentuate rather than soften. Rameses and Sulla would have approved this city as employment, but Hitler Speer and Saddam would have felt at home here. Drab in the central shadows of the middle distance behind some faceless basilica stands a melancholy young woman clasping a naked infant to her shoulder.
      Before the muted background Poussin defines his actors, vivid in primary colors and animated ire. At left a haggard caitiff slyly slinks from out the frame as a malice-snarled condoner smirks his gestured quick vale. The chief Pharisee in saffron shiftlessly expounds as defensively he gestures to Him he would ensnare. Twisted faces, angry gestures, nervous postures deform the left-hand tableau as the male vigilantes canvass The Arbiter of Doom. At right a

frightened witness drags his confused companion to quit the place of Judgment ere complicity succeeds. Beside them stoop earnest and quizzing faces hurriedly consulting and pointing to the dust. Right of center stands Our Savior pointing with calm composure to the pudic hand of a woman kneeling dishevelled and forlorn.

Poussin splits his canvas equally with a louring vinculum along which he deploys the eyes of all the active protagonists and also the young mother in the middle distant shadows. Whilst the vertical ratio of The Face of Christ is thus 1:1, the horizontal ratio is apparently 5:3 (measuring from the left). More careful study will, however, justify a significant revision of this latter Pythagorean measure. The face of the chief Pharisee coincides with the arris of the looming basilica against the sky with a horizontal 1:2 ratio. It is not easy to discover Phidian structure in this canvas and its simple arithmetic ratios and bold straight lineaments remind one of sacred scenes by other hands. And yet closer scrutiny fixes The Heart of Christ at $\varphi:1$ in the horizontal and nearly $\varphi:1$ in the vertical. The fact that the central balustrade ramp is not on a perfect diagonal from bottom left to top right but is offset parallel to the existing diagonal furnishes strong evidence of cropping and The Heart may well have been drafted at $\varphi:1$. Once again it is clear that Poussin regarded the famous transcendental number (not mathematically-appreciated as transcendental in his time) as the co-ordinate of the situs of Sacred Love which he counterposed with profane agency at a rational intersection.

Poussin presents all the menace and confrontation of the great Johannine narrative with the tension of the eyeline and confinement of the prospect. But he awards centrality not to Christ but to the unregarded mother and baby in the background, for that centrality is what He who died for all our generations awarded them. Is the mother the reproof and the justification of The Law? She has nothing to say but is the scene's most eloquent witness.

Here men are on top and command sternly. There is oppression but also acceptance and rejection. For it is not Life that is rejected but The Law, as in the acceptance of Sin men and women grasp the Seeds of Salvation.

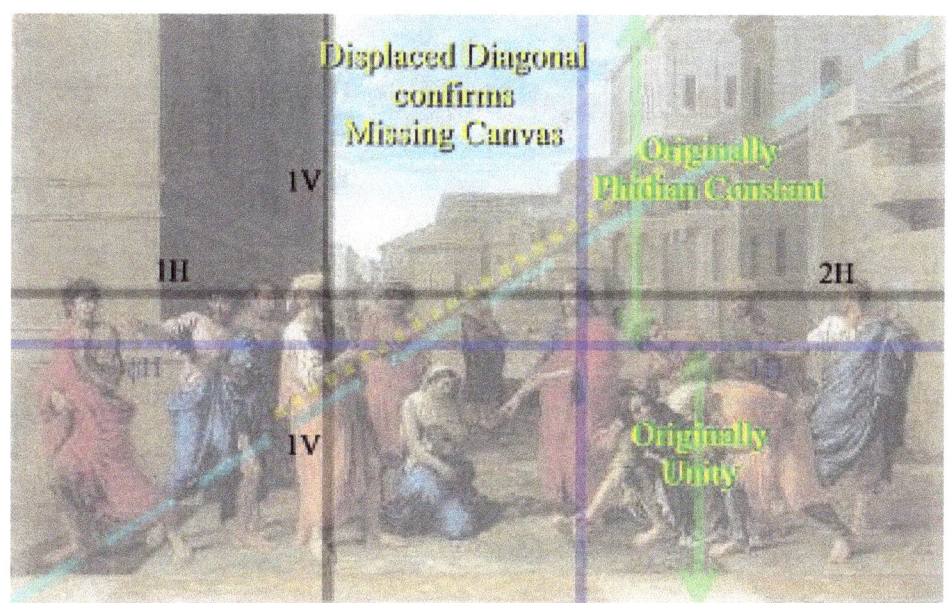

**Explanatory Illustration for the Analysis
of "Christ and the Woman Taken in Adultery"**

Bibliography and References

1. "Landscape Painting"
   Bo Jeffares
   The Phaidon Press of Oxford   1979
   ISBN 0-7148-1985-9

2. "Nicolas Poussin (1594-1665)"
   Richard Verdi
   Zwemmer of London   1995
   ISBN 0-302-00647-8

   a. Also known as:-
   "The Finding of Moses, 1638"
   Museé de Louvre
   Départment des Peintures
   Paris

   b. "The Arcadian Shepherds, 1638-40"
   Museé de Louvre
   Départment des Peintures
   Paris

   c. "Landscape with the Body of Phocion Carried out of Athens, 1648"
   The National Museum of Wales
   Cardiff

   d. "Landscape with the Ashes of Phocion Collected by his Widow, 1648"
   The Walker Art Gallery
   Liverpool

   e. "Christ and the Woman taken in Adultery, 1653"
   Museé de Louvre
   Départment des Peintures
   Paris

The Tree of Snails

3-10 May 1998

We know little of the Old Testament prophet Isaiah. Saul, David and Solomon were near contemporaries of Homer, Agamemnon and the heroes of Archaic Greece whose deeds and works have abundantly come down to us. Isaiah and the kings he served lived from 750-700BC in the ancient Dark Age that for us intercalates six hundred blank pages between the Heroic and the Periclean.

Clearly Isaiah was a man of affairs in the thick of Semitic politics of which he provides a few lugubrious glimpses. His gentle view of animals lends him an immediate sympathy to myself and many other late twentieth-century readers. The celebrated Eleventh Chapter of Isaiah praises The Peaceable Kingdom and this alone has made him an old Quaker favorite who inspired the brushes of American Primitives like Edward Hicks as well as allied Romantics such as Blake.

Animals play their innocent part in his vibrant chiaroscuro of Good and Evil as the ringing Promises of God reverberate through the timeless majesty of pages that no transliterative banality can mar. In this last respect Isaiah shares the tone of The Gospels, in which the reader senses, in whatever sorry rendition, that a god is speaking. And it is of course for his strange adumbrations of the earthly journey of Our Savior that he has been retained in the Christian canon.

April the Twenty-Eighth 1998. The manageress of my Wife's club telephones Jana. Would she like to join in a dance round the maypole on Mayday? My Wife is a good gymnast but a better Catholic and decides to take a rain check on that one. I am not an expert on maypoles but I understand that two contrarotating arbors surmount the pole and that dancers process in opposing circuits, though should the arbors bind the dancers spiral to the tree. I am not sure that I understand the ritual meaning of this, if any. One is compellingly reminded of the concentric and spiral designs carved upon megalithic tombs in Ireland and elsewhere, some of which may date to 3000BC. I have it on authority that such geometries are conjured in the shamanic hallucinations induced to this day and reflected in ethnic art. Whatever the case, concentric and spiraling figures are allied and are very ancient conceptions.

Christianity came late to Mercia and was not welcome. Even after one thousand years the attitude of the local people to the new religion remains ambiguous. I work in a town whose name still celebrates the chief of the old gods whose fane crowned the hill guarding the center of England as his name still centers the English week. Hopkins and other nasty witch-finders prospered upon this plateau, but even now lurid rumors persist of waifs as diverse as Nazi parachutists and black mares suffering lethal ill-use in night-sequestered coverts. Readers "of a certain age" possibly recollect Meon Hill and the notorious crime that baffled Fabian of the Yard.

May the First 1998. A cold North wind blew down the Southernmost Pennine scarps shimmering the unkempt locks of ungrazed grass whose polished blades glanced like squall-stroked ripples in the sunlight. Further afield the Friesians of dandelion-dotted pastures sheltered behind the drystone dykes as lambs and ewes hunkered in the growth. In the valley below the walled and glaucous lawns of The White Peak yielded to the hawthorn hedges of Midland meadows.

The long-lorn hummocks of two short straight rakes showed where men had grazed for lead. But all flesh is grass[a] and the flesh that stays grazes without bruising.

Jana, Sung Woo and I returned along the gentle grade of the old railway to Tissington. At Alsop-en-le-Dale we entered a sheltered cutting in the limestone and found a young and lissom birch sprouted beside the trackbed. Its sturdy young trunk and slender branches seemed to crop at random from their feral substrate like facts that happen without reason but are solid none the less.

At first we admired what seemed no more than our favorite tree, the paper-barked Silver Birch[b]. As our eyes grew accustomed to its peeling integument we found to our astonishment a graceful snail clinging at eye-level to the trunk. Then we saw another and presently descried a dozen or a score also populating the branches. All sorts of snails. Some sported Great Western livery of chocolate and cream as they recycled the Dinantian[c] in their perfect air-spun volutes. Some of these silent creatures had straw and silver swirls like the etiolated grass of winter to grace their tender backs. Why they climbed so far to such heady extremities was not immediately clear. But presently we detected lush and virid fields of epiphytic algae clinging to the bark. The little molluscs did not, however, graze these preferring to harvest more recondite herbage invisible to us.

Below the spreading branches some of the tiny toilers bestrewed the ground. Some were set at nought by gusts that had dislodged them as they essayed to cross smooth ground or the precarious traverses of undersides. Others had been torn from their Eiger by little raptors who had winkled them outwith.

Did the snails know that this birch was one of many, and that there were an almost infinite diversity of other substrates different in kind? Did they know of the far stars above or the distant sea or the exotic lands beyond? Were they aware that although all birches share a common program that no two are alike in their phenogenesis?

The snails strived to feed of the tree. They evolved the splendid symmetries of their shells from the disordered substance of its lawns, each *decus et tutamen*.

Each one of us grazes a tree of experience upon which we elaborate the structure of theory, our guide, our ornament, our shield.

But as fall the snails so the theories of men. Some plummet almost silently as they negotiate the slippery undersides of conjecture as phlogiston fell to the ice-shod clockwork of the young Davy. Some fall to a swift and silent swoop from the screaming skies like the geocentric epicycles of Ptolemy to the revolution of Copernicus; and their fragile spirals strew the dust with gaudy splinters. For all evolution is theory and all theories evolutions. God did not ask whether Huxley's grandmother was an ape or else his grandfather, for God knew that Huxley's mum and dad were *both* apes, and knew that we are all God's Children; and God is no monkey.

But God may have said:-

"The carpenter stretcheth out his rule; he marketh it out with a line; he fitteth it with planes, and he marketh it out with the compass, and maketh it after the figure of a man, according to the beauty of a man; that it may remain in the house. He heweth him down cedars, and taketh the cypress and the oak, which he strengtheneth for himself among the trees of the forest: he planteth an ash, and the rain doth nourish it. Then shall it be for a man to burn: for he will take thereof, and warm himself; yea, he kindleth it, and baketh bread; yea, he maketh a god, and worshippeth it; he maketh it a graven image, and falleth down thereto."[d]

I do not know what furtive creature had assaulted the broken or winkled snails but I blame thrushes. So in ecological parlance the snail is prey and the thrush is predator. Allow that M is the Number of Snails in a closed community and that N is the Number of Thrushes. b is the Birth Rate of Snails and d their Death Rate. r is their Rate of Increase b-d. z is the Death Rate of Thrushes.

The mutual Rates of Change of the coexisting Predator-Prey populations are dynamic and are expressed by the interacting Lotka Equations[1]:-

$$\frac{dM}{dt} = rM - kMN$$
$$\frac{dN}{dt} = jMN - zN$$

Do not worry if you do not understand the mathematics of this illustration: I am not *au fait* with simultaneous differential equations myself[e]. The point is that these arcane objects are mere intimations of reality, shadows upon the walls of Plato's Cave, symbols with which man models a tree and those who live in its shade. By inspection of the two formulae you can appreciate their complementarity and their chiastic symmetry, but I doubt you shall be mesmerised by these for the symbolic system, a gross oversimplification derived from naïve assumptions, will in any case lose further reality in the process of solution.

We wish to track the fortunes of the two contending tribes of Snail and Thrush through time but technically this can only be achieved via a power series expansion of the activity constant k, a process which is necessarily approximate, but whose precision can be chosen *a priori* to yield radically different forecasts.

If you neglect higher order terms in your expansion the two populations wrestle in (M,N) space to oscillate through infinitely-repeated ellipsoidal cycles of complementary boom and bust as they chase each other round a very strange attractor. Take a few more power series terms into play and the forecast is very different: The two tribes spiral through damped cycles to an equilibrium point in which the numbers of Snails and Thrushes maintain a fixed ratio.

Three hundred years ago men fancied the cool measures of mathematics reflected The Plan of God for His Eternal Creation, and their conceit intensified until the days of Hilbert. By the time that Volterra and Lotka wrote in 1925, the foundering of the Titanic and the bloody morass of The Great War had shaken the belief of men in their ability to descry the Purposes of the Deity or indeed in His very Existence. And yet the feeling lingered that He should not be tempted.

And what elegance and what symmetry and what order can mirror the pain the blood and the fear of Predator and Prey locked into timeless cycles of death and contention?

Perhaps our obscure Iron Age advisor feels that he has another Message to relay:-

"For my thoughts are not your thoughts, neither are your ways my ways, saith the LORD. For as the heavens are higher than the earth, so are my ways higher than your ways, and my thoughts than your thoughts."[f]

Notes

- a   Isaiah 40:6
- b   Betula Pendula: an aspen-like European tree that colonises waste land and well-drained upland moors
- c   a massively-bedded, frequently plumbiferous marine limestone of the Lower Carboniferous
- d   Isaiah 44:13,15
- e   The Lotka Equations were originally configured for the mathematically-identical instance of entomological parasitism. They are a simplified specialisation of The Volterra Equations (due to Vito Volterra) which are differential equations of the Velhulstian growth logistic. The Volterra Equations are meant to describe general interspecific competition.
- f   Isaiah 55:8,9

References

1. "Elements of Physical Biology"
   Alfred J Lotka
   Williams and Wilkins Company of Baltimore
   1925

Children of God

29 July 1998

The God that holds you over the pit of hell, much as one holds a spider or some loathsome insect over the fire, abhors you and is dreadfully provoked. His wrath towards you burns like fire; he looks upon you as worthy of nothing else, but to be cast into the fire; he is of purer eyes than to bear to have you in his sight; you are ten thousand times more abominable in his eyes than the most hateful venomous serpent is in ours. You have offended him infinitely more than ever a stubborn rebel did his prince - and yet it is nothing but his hand that holds you from falling into the fire every moment.

So avers the argent prose and leaden promise of the eighteenth-century American revivalist Jonathan Edwards[1].
Here in Britain we have a tiny but very venomous creature called the money spider[a], whom old superstition calls the harbinger of wealth. With unfathomable wisdom he parachutes in on a strand of gossamer to build his hammocks on my lawn where only the dew of a summer's morn will betray his handiwork. Christ tells us that fowls do not gather into barns[b] neither lilies spin[c] but the money spider is a master fabricant though arachnologists must reach for their microscopes to examine his brain.
On the sunlit lawns of my Sussex kindergarten flirtatious little girls exclaimed "Jimmy, Jimmy, you've got a money spider" as they retrieved the barely visible black globule of life from my hair, whilst he shinned up his phantom rope to nestle on their flesh. Though eminently capable he did not bite. What Guardian assured him that he was arrested by the sportive hands of infants, and should presently be delivered? Did hot little hands burn him like fire yet remain unprovoked?
Some years ago I read of laborers digging the sludge from a settling pond in a Midland sewage farm on a sultry Mercian day much like this. Suddenly an entire airborne division of these tiny spiders landed on their naked backs and bit so voraciously that those hardy men ceased work immediately and sought medical assistance. No lasting damage was done (at least to humans!) but what prompted these little voyagers to deploy their only weapon in circumstances with so little promise of profit? Money spiders have done nothing to defray my debt but I owe them something.
My Korean wife considers England a demiparadise and told her relatives that "even the animals are gentle", but three of our species have known

lethality. Two or three summers ago Jana and I walked down an overgrown path on Cannock Chase when I froze as I heard a disembodied hiss. I looked down to see a stout old viper[d] coiled beside my left shin. Jana wisely ran down the brae but I was too close to risk a sudden movement. The venomous serpent reared to strike and the gaunt black barb of his head looked hard and satanic as he abhorred the loathsome surprise above him. Then I said defensively "Hello, snake, don't you hiss at *me*" whereupon he hastened across my path and disappeared into the bracken. After my brief St Patrick act I wondered whether the snake could not bear to have me in his hearing or whether he was truly reassured. By me? No? Then by whom?

The second killer is very different. As an undergraduate I undertook geological mapping alone amongst the rocky splendor of the Atholl Highlands. Sometimes I would look up from my outcrops to watch the stately herds of red deer[e] process in silence behind magnificently-antlered stags as, ignoring me, they patrolled the windswept fastnesses of their range. Wealthy "sportsmen" dreadfully provoke these princes and sometimes themselves quit the hill aback a garron.

A few days ago my Father and I drove to Invermark for a walk up the glen beside Loch Lee. We admired the superb fibrous iron fenestration of the ruined castle at the wayside but were less impressed by the extempore gunloops driven through the walls by the Home Guard. Some loops commanded the eastern valley approach from Strathmore and the sea but others pointed westward into the mountains. I said to my Father "surely they could not have expected the Nazis to come from *there*?" and he speculated that they might have had paratroops in mind. I said "would *you* drop men into that rock-strewn hell up there?".

The future is fantasy. When we prepare our defence it is in anticipation of evil that may not merely fail to ensue, but may even be impossible. Perhaps we share Jonathan's preoccupation with conscience at the expense of paying consciousness due regard. For our apprehension of danger is conditioned by the level of our understanding as well as our faulty expectation of our enemy. Perhaps this is what Satan learned when after the Forty Days he abandoned Christ to the wilderness[f]. We cannot despise the spider for mistaking his predicament or the snake for his change of tactics when we ourselves spend centuries against legions who never march.

Further up the glen my Father and I found a tiny graveyard above the placid hill-girt lake. The high dry-stane walls shelter a roofless kirk and the sleeping generations from the roaring Highland winds remitted that day. Saplings had been planted to replace the great trees that the elders of the parish had nurtured in the days when meager harvests supported a peasantry. Beyond, the peaty waters of the loch riffled in the breeze with the unctuous gleam that a diffused sun confers upon standing water in these oblique latitudes. On the ancient tombstones within were graven the skulls and scapulae with which ancient Scottish custom betokened death. The small plain sandstone tablets of feudal times were rudely carved with what earnest "Irish" tribesmen fancied to be English orthography whilst their skulls were cartoon faces and their bones like steerage oars. Father thought they were carved by kin of the deceased. In vital contrast the local dominie, buried a mere thirty years later, had a refined slab of freestone whose precise North British Letters were framed with *momenti mori* of grim Hunterian realism. The iron gates were open and a ewe and lamb grazed the lush lawns of the graveyard. As we entered the ewe left and the lamb became agitated upon loosing sight of her. Father tried to maneuver him toward the gate but, because I was near the gate, the lamb panicked and ran to the other side of the enclosure where he and his mother disconsolately exchanged bleats through the wall. He was unable to perceive the exit to reunion even when I left the vicinity. It was as if, knowing what he wanted and being in full communion with it, his fear and forgetfulness had robbed him of the means.

    As we left the churchyard to walk beside the lake we saw distantly ahead on the track a group of brightly-anoraked people milling about shouting and throwing stones in the water. They did not seem of childish stature and I contemplated with trepidation our passage through such a pack of yobs. As Father and I drew into the midst of these people their disengaged manners and mongoloid faces clarified that they were idiots, and far from being yobs those capable gave us kindly smiles and civil greetings. I call them "idiots" because to be an idiot is wholly honorable and a condition to be respected. It may be true that their facility at (say) inferential statistics is not as developed as mine but are you going to sneer at me because I never mastered the art of the Laplace transform? Am I accordingly "a person with learning difficulties" or perhaps a "mentally-challenged person"? You did not measure the cognition of the money spider or the lamb by your own standards though you may feel justified in classifying me as a "less ontologically able person" or even a "failed academic". Such circumlocutions are valid enough but you would question the value and relevancy of such apophatic descriptions and as God holds the both of us over the pit of hell will he measure us by our own yardsticks, or by His Perfect Measure, or judge us as what we truly are?

After sharing lunch near the bridge at the head of Loch Lee, my Father and I briskly returned to the car park at Invermark. The council had planted a young rowan[g] on a grass verge and a very obese cock chaffinch bobbed beneath, like a little ball of mauve-pink knitting wool. As we neared the car large flocks of pastel cocks settled in expectant silence and bobbed around us with the odd dun hen. Towards the rear of one flight a single chaffinch thought I may have overlooked their presence and uttered a brief squeak. I said "What do you mean?:- squeak" as I broke some water biscuits and scattered the voracious crumbs. It seemed to me that parents were taking a well-earned refreshment between frantic bouts of feeding insectivorous children and I prayed for their safety and their success. Father told me to marshal the birds aside whilst he reversed the car over the crumbs but the flock disappeared aloft at the first movement, doubtless to re-alight on our departure.

Edwards asks us to see ourselves as our own worst fears: The insidious, venomous, easily-overlooked enemy against which an ape has no defence, for his defence is predicated upon the visible, the physical and the predictable. The Darwinian and similar mechanistic paradigms of creation tend to "explain" the nature and origin of creatures in terms of adaptive selection. Like all models of reality this is fine as long as it is not extrapolated beyond the reaches of tenability. But it seems to me that such models falter when one considers the operations of *compensation* and of *choice*. The money spider shares a strange condition with the notorious Black Widow[i]; the European Viper; and with Man himself:- He is naked. Whereas most spiders and many other animals are protected by a rich pile of urticaceous hairs or long sharp teeth these vulnerable creatures need possess and deploy venomous wrath. Contrast the glabrous spiders with a potent but dozy creature like the Mexican Red-Kneed Tarantula who is as hispid as a hedgehog[j] and just as complacent. Boys attempt to keep both species as pets and can do so safely. For sure, you can explain alternative defensive adaptations mechanistically if you are prepared to defy Occam[k] and draw a very long bow. But I think that choice remains a problem for mechanistic schemes. Why does an animal whose neurological capacity for dexterity or decision seems so inadequate build a hammock on grass but not brick, or bite a workman but spare a child?

Isaiah promised us that one day beyond time the suckling infant would play by the hole of the asp and the weaned child place his hand on the cockatrice' den with impunity[l]. Perhaps he foresaw a sentient state in which the mundane imperatives to feed or become food would be redundant.

Maybe God needs no fires because His pure eyes discern the Essence in Ways to which partial eyes, whether two or eight, are blind. *We* need fires to refine our ideas for we know that in the base regulus of thought there is often a refulgent silver bead that will trickle to the cupel as the dross and litharge blows from our cupola's hearth.

Notes

a	A black glabrous arachnid of the Linyphia family. Leg spread varies from about one to two millimeters.
b	Matthew 6:26
c	Matthew 6:28
d	*Vipera Berus*: A viviparous basking snake up to 65 cms long having dark zigzag markings along its back. Known in Britain as the "adder" it has there occasioned six human fatalities since 1900. There are no Irish snakes: According to legend St Patrick expelled them.
e	*Cervus Elaphus*: A horse-sized tawny ungulate common on uncultivated uplands which have occasional tree cover.
f	Matthew 4:1,11
g	*Sorbus Aucuparia*: A silver-barked deciduous tree of acid upland soils which grows up to five meters tall
h	*Fringilla Coelebs*: A gregarious, usually silent European passerine. Cock has distinctive mauve-pink breast feathers.
i	*Latrodéctus Máctans*: A glabrous American arachnid. The larger and more venomous female has occasioned eighty-eight human fatalities since 1620.
j	*Erinaceous Europaeus*: A spiny insectivore mammal of European undergrowth. Adult length twenty to thirty centimeters.
k	William of Occam or Ockham (c1290-1349) English Franciscan nominalist who introduced The Rule of Parsimony, or as he put it "accidentals should not be multiplied beyond necessity".
l	Isaiah 11:8

Reference

1. "The Lion Concise Book of Christian Thought"
   Tony Lane   1996
   Lion Publishing plc of Oxford
   ISBN 0-7459-3702-0

Can Quakers Grasp the Nettle?
An Attender Enquires

29 August 1998

I read with fascination Alastair Heron's article of QF Volume A:Part 4 and I will start by addressing his last point since it is the least problematical: A "Friend" or "Quaker" is a man or woman who will walk unarmed onto a battlefield to ameliorate suffering because "[Spirituality is] attention to values deriving from other than material self-interest" to borrow William Spray's golden quotation. Whilst we all hope that no-one shall ever again take that test we note its satisfaction tells nothing of the candidate's real or alleged "pacifism" or even "Christianity".

Quaker Catholics Confuse Newcomer

Clearly literal battlegrounds may be of fortuitous or factitious genesis whilst figurative ones may be "no more than" command floors aboard "the spaceship of the imagination".

So the above definition, should it be valid, evidently affords a catholic conception of Quakerhood that would include *et al* Galileo, Huxley, both Wilberforces and at least one of the Saints Ignatius, not to mention The Desert Fathers. For Quaker is as Quaker does, not as Quaker says, and to those who protest that disputants and anchorites indulge in ego-trips I reply that he who wagers hide and Soul for Truth (no matter how misconceived) is an altruist.

Complacency Challenged

I consider that Alastair's work in canvassing and analysing the views of Members and Attenders in Yorkshire is a key method in the identification of reasons for the nexus of difficulties associated with Membership and the decline of The (British) Religious Society of Friends, and as such is a necessary predicate of reform. Alastair's foresight and intelligent industry warrants thanks and gratitude.

A historicising and retrospective view must however be extended into a strategic prospectus if recovery is to be prosecuted. Like any human institution the Society is "twelve monkeys in a sack" but it is a distinctive contribution to our poor simian civilisation and the world would be a sorrier place without it.

Shall we discuss some of the problems and propose some potential remedies?

Constitutional Difficulties

With due apologies to QF readers (and of course Immanuel Kant) Quakers must decide upon what they are and where they stand by resolving their disparate ideas into two groups:-

(a) Categorical Values

These are "core" precepts to which all members would be asked to assent and which should be the basis of the Society's advertised, public manifesto.

For instance, Members may elect to adopt "pacifism" as a core value, or to take a definite (affirmative or negative) policy on "total abstinence". At this level they must also grasp the nettle over whether they are exclusively Christian or whether atheists, Buddhists and other spiritually-interested people will continue to be welcome.

(b) Hypothetical Values

These are "marginal" precepts about which the Society has no policy and includes concepts such as "myths to be exploded", archaic practices, unhelpful administrative procedures and any other ideological luxury that deters enquirers or alienates potential sympathisers. Such presumably includes the "hat honor" to which Alastair adverts but also much more serious matters such as the non-existence of balloting procedures within the Society.

It is very remarkable (and in my view very laudable) that Quakers have no creed but this is not to say that practical, modern, attractive positions cannot be embraced in The Light of the Teachings of The Living Christ and perhaps those of other Prophets and Masters.

Many old institutions are turning their human fortunes round by bravely confronting their tradition and adopting promises and projects that speak to the modern condition. The Labour Party is of course a spectacular example but I believe that The Quakers can attract and hold a vast new constituency of humane but disaffected people seething around out there in today's morally-rarefied atmosphere, and what is more they can do this without compromising the religious or moral integrity of their great old faith.

As a trades unionist I candidly tell you that such a change in the Society's nature and projection would be painful and acrimonious in its execution, carrying the danger of schism, but men and women of good will can change themselves and change organisations whilst remaining loyal to one another and building for the needs of tomorrow.

Analytical Methods and Planned Publicity

Alastair's model of garnering and processing data about "consumer satisfaction" is tedious and expensive, in money time and pride, but his courageous inception of such analysis must be picked up and developed if Quakers are not to join the Ranters and the Albigenses in the footnotes of church history: Quakers deserve more because they think the rest of us deserve.

It is pointless for The Society of Friends to advertise their existence in newspapers or other media without prior identification of their strengths and weaknesses, not as *objectively* extant (for no human knows what such may be) but as *subjectively* apprehended by the public. Such prior discoveries would be an indispensable basis of, not mere defensive "myth-busting", but active intelligently-addressed pursuit of potential members.

To Quakers who think this is very well for marketing toothpaste or Sonic but not The Fellowship in God I say this: Today's man or woman *needs* God more than cleanliness just as today's child needs fellowship more than Sega. And to those who regard proselytisation with understandable distaste I say that good truthful publicity will reduce the frustrations and disappointments that disillusioned enquirers take away with them.

Some Personal Observations

In the appendix on Page 11, Alastair Heron highlights some interesting if disturbing statistics. In approximation, 47% of the 56 million Britons claim to be Christian and 6% of 56 million are regular attenders of Christian gatherings. Accordingly Alastair's 26381 Quakers represent about 0.8% of "practicing Christians". I should presume that grossly understates the proportion of "center-left" religious people of all colors and classes who are the Quakers' natural constituency. But some of the interpretations implied may not be the natural extrapolations they would seem at first sight, for though only some

65.7% of practicing Quakers are "card-carrying members" they are not wholly burdened with "upkeep of meetings" since many Attenders are glad to furnish both financial and practical help at local, and even international, levels. Perhaps this last reminds us that Quakerism is a Sacred Mission, not just a gentleman's' (and gentlewoman's') club or an organisation where frustrated bureaucrats can play at being committee men in their spare time. For sure, quite a few people haunt churches (or any places of social resort) to gratify vanity or frivolity but most Quakers I have met and all at my meeting are kindly, helpful, idealistic, forbearing and generous men and women. Though they are cheerful and entirely unpretentious there are local meetings where a somewhat smug and bourgeois atmosphere can greet the visitor. The unfortunate result of this is that it is possible to attend a Monthly Meeting of one hundred and see no black, Asian or obviously working-class person in a part of Europe where 6% are Afro-Caribbean, 12% Subcontinental and (locally) 97% CDE. I accept that Quakerism has long been a "safe haven" for "middle-class intellectuals" who become, or wish to remain, Christian. But this in no manner diminishes its potential for good any more than it tarnishes Friends' illustrious history. What it does imply is that you (dare I say "we"?) need to adjust your ways to the by-no-means-wholly-evil exigencies of new times.

It is sad to think that some might not join for "no commitment unless necessary to get what you want" reasons for it seems that the entire point of joining a religious group is to serve Christ (or your god) as opposed to Self. I can however understand "difficulty of knowing what they would be joining". Without specious representation of representativeness let me conclude by sharing the two major impediments to my seeking membership: One is doctrinal, the other political:-

(1) The Light Within
This is a very big stumblingblock for someone who happens to know Christ is exogenous, because he was befriended by Christ when he had exhausted his private intellectual and moral powers, and was personally rescued (instrumentally by an enemy) during a specific episode.

(2) The Absence of Modern Voting Systems
I am a member of several political, university and scientific organisations, UK and US, in all of which I have voting rights even though those are seldom exercised.

I have reason to think that Christ influences the outcome of elections but whether or not that is so I consider democracy to be wholly consistent with the aspirations of the historic Quaker mission.

I think you are fine people, much better than I, and I want your Society to strengthen and grow for the sake of Peace in Christ.

The Voyage of the Sigismondo

15 October 1998

Today we grope to interpret the radiological emissions of the scattered stars and to unscramble the mathematical message of the gathered genome. We geologists know what it is to doubt, to quest and to be confused. I can sense the beauty and the grandeur of the part-seen splendors about me and yet I struggle in vain to frame the phrase that expresses my puny understanding, for I have not the words to match the wonder nor the wit to comprehend it.

Join my Father and I on a balmy island beach at midnight. The sand is black. The sea is black. The sheer mountain before us is black and looming. Cicadas sing from the tussocks to sweethearts they have never beheld, and yet seem assured are there for the courting. But my poor Father can no longer hear them, though he knows they must be there.

We are in a world of sound without sight and of sight without sound.

Far from the distant summit comes a fleeting glow of red reflected upon the flimsy awning of mist above. Occasionally silent white sparks describe their steep parabolas as if Vulcan himself were smiting a kindling flint as Aeolus blew his damp and salty tinder[1]. Obliquely down the hillside process dancing lines of flashlights as the descending files of trekkers pick their paths across the scoria[2].

The bars of San Vincenzo have closed but close at hand a saffron garland of sodium lamps marks the jetty where the adze-hewn timbers of the motor ketch[3] Sigismondo await to cradle our party across the warm and rocking sea. We board the little ship. I understand that she was built to star with Ingrid Bergman in the film "Stromboli". She now rides against the eponymous volcano. Often these filmic scenes flickered in the dark and were gone. Tonight we shall view other stars. Maybe an hour later our tired comrades straggle in silence across the gunwale. Like black vestiges of the gay Italian sunset they stand or sit or lie a charmed tableau.

I had earlier remarked to my Father how little livestock graced the Sicilian landscape and the previous Tuesday I was accordingly rather surprised to discover five sheep in the shade of the Southern cliff in a remote ravine on Lipari. They must not have quite astonished me as the herd of pigs amazed Our Savior and the other good Jews who strode with Him along another slope above a different sea so long ago.

Matthew relates the unforgettable tale in these terms:-

> And when he was come to the other side into the country of the Gergesenes, there met him two possessed with devils, coming out of the tombs, exceeding fierce, so that no man might pass by that way. And, behold, they cried out, saying, What have we to do with thee, Jesus, thou Son of God? art thou come hither to torment us before the time? And there was a good way off from them an herd of many swine feeding. So the devils besought him, saying, If thou cast us out, suffer us to go away into the herd of swine. And he said unto them, Go. And when they were come out, they went into the herd of swine: and, behold, the whole herd of swine ran violently down a steep place into the sea, and perished in the waters.[a]

What are we to make of this strange report and the weird stratagem described? No where else do The Gospels suggest that Christ was callous in his view of or actions towards animals: If anything somewhat the contrary:-

> Are not two sparrows sold for a farthing? and one of them shall not fall on the ground without your Father.[b]

Fortunately Luke supplies a more complete and much more disturbing account of this famous episode:-

> And they arrived at the country of the Gadarenes, which is over against Galilee. And when he went forth to land, there met him out of the city a certain man, which had devils a long time, and ware no clothes, neither abode in any house, but in the tombs. When he saw Jesus, he cried out, and fell down before him, and with a loud voice said, What have I to do with thee, Jesus, thou Son of God most high? I beseech thee, torment me not. (For he had commanded the unclean spirit to come out of the man. For oftentimes it had caught him: and he was kept bound with chains and in fetters; and he brake the bands, and was driven of the devil into the wilderness.) And Jesus asked him, saying, What is thy name? And he said, Legion: because many devils were entered into him. And they besought him that he would not command them to go out into the deep. And there was there an herd of many swine feeding on the mountain: and they besought him that he would suffer them to enter into them. And he suffered them. Then went the devils out of the man, and entered into the swine: and the herd ran violently down a steep place into the lake, and were choked.[c]

What are we to make of this strange report and the weird stratagem described? No where else do The Gospels suggest that Christ was cunning or insidious: If anything somewhat the contrary:-

And in the fourth watch of the night Jesus went unto them, walking on the sea. And when the disciples saw him walking on the sea, they were troubled, saying, It is a spirit; and they cried out for fear. But straightway Jesus spake unto them, saying, Be of good cheer; it is I; be not afraid. And Peter answered him and said, Lord, if it be thou, bid me come unto thee on the water. And he said, Come. And when Peter was come down out of the ship, he walked on the water, to go to Jesus. But when he saw the wind boisterous, he was afraid; and beginning to sink, he cried, saying, Lord, save me. And immediately Jesus stretched forth his hand, and caught him, and said unto him, O thou of little faith, wherefore didst thou doubt?[d]

The Sigismondo rounds the dark and sleeping cone of Stromboli and points a ponent heading across the softly rippled surface. The throb of the diesels measures our passage as all other sounds subside on this soporific sea. Alice appears and stands in motionless silhouette beneath her broad-brimmed black hat like that caped caballero on the old wine bottles or like some tutelary genius of the helm. Strange dark creatures break surface forward the beam as like God-appointed pilots they guide us landward.

The constellations crowd the pellucid sky. The Milky Way appears as a great larboard[4] pathway whilst a declined Plow lights our starboard[5] beam. Still the ghostly white of the bowsprit points our plodding course against the sussurating breeze, as below amidst the white foam of the bow-wave soft electric blue circles of phosphorescent jellyfish pave the sea with sapphire. Gerald exclaims in delighted amazement but I am rapt in speechless wonder at our noctilucent world. Presently we discern fleeting sparks of barium and magnesium[6] as littler creatures flush in alarm but I trust not trauma to the pressure of the prow. For these modest children have also found safety in The Triumph of the Light[7]. In the Northern sky a shooting star seeks to emulate a coelenterate with its evanescent streak of fire.

Sitting ahead in the atrament the faraglione[8] of Basiluzzo and Lisca Bianca present the jagged backs of lava specters, their washed pastels of sunlit tricolore[9] all the same in the silver starlight as they frame our homeward portal.

I wrestle for days with the awe and beauty of this experience pondering the nature and meaning of the Message advertised. Something, or maybe Someone, draws me back to those parallel passages about The Gadarene Swine.

Consider again that unique Lucan phrase:-

And they besought him that he would not command them to *go out into the deep.*[e]

What a world is lost in Matthew's careless omission!

Christ, Luke clarifies, agreed that the devils need not submerge. He acceded to their preference. But both Parties reckoned without the Will of the pigs. The swine voted with their feet and the devils won what they most feared after all. God made a mistake, and God could not retrieve it.

I do not believe that men can truly understand God. I do believe that it is fatuous to credit (or blame) God for providing our environment, because it is clear that He did not manufacture the firmament or install its physical genotypes in any of the vulgar senses of creation that we can understand. If God, in some metaphysical sense beyond our ken, primed the universe and sent it on its way then it is like the clockwork toy that a child wound and set a birling down a cobbled brae only to watch it bounce and saltate uncatchably to an unforeseen station.

God still however cares for the living creatures of His Realm and He will step in to Aid them when He can which is when we rightly ask Him. It is in this sense, locally and specially, yet out of time and space, that God and Man defy gravity.

<u>Readings</u>

a   Matthew 8:28;32
b   Matthew 10:29
c   Luke   8:26;33
d   Matthew 14:25;31
e   Luke   8:31

Explanatory Notes

1. Vulcan and Aeolus: Respectively the Roman gods of forges and the wind
2. Volcanic rubble
3. A small two-masted sailing vessel, often with auxiliary power
4. On the left-hand side with reference to the prow
5. On the right-hand side with reference to the prow
6. Barium and Magnesium: Two metals used to color fireworks respectively green and white
7. Sigismondo is the Italian form of the Germanic name Sigismund, literally "victory-protection" or "safety through triumph"
8. Sea-stacks
9. The Italian national flag of red, white and green: The porous volcanic rock of The Aeolian Islands frequently shows a subdued form of that scheme when leeched by spray and rain

The Shining Embassy of Alopen

24 October 1998

Alopen stood upon the bluff above the river as the screaming dust[a] immersed the looming city in a lake of limonitic yellow beneath a cobalt sky. The setting sun behind him cast an etiolated light upon the gilded towers and temples whose mundic[b] gleam relieved the shaly blackness of the darkling town ahead.

Beside the watercourses the dusty swords of phragmitic grasses seemed to flail in frantic opposition to the glaucous spears of willows as silent files of peasants picked their way along the dykes. Dogs barked against the wind whilst shy children hid behind the doors of hovels as the asses and the camel tossed their heads in tinkling harness and snorted hair-fringed muffles against the choking air-borne silt. Before him the urban scumble stretched beyond the mighty ship-strewn confluence as far as eye could see. As Alopen watched and waited baleful lamps began to puncture the vast diorama as if to foil with flecks of gold the silver stars above.

Ahead in Xanadu[c], the greatest city on Earth, chaos enveloped the Court. Who was the babbling stranger whose sudden outlandish appearance perturbed the new-found serenity of the Middle Kingdom? Clearly he was not a person on business from Porlock[d]. His fair skin and frankish features could mean only one thing, too incredible to contemplate.

For centuries, the learned and the surd all regaled their children with fantastic tales of the Empire of Ta-ch'in, which was likely to exist only as The Antipodes, an allegorical counterpoise to the weight of the world. For the truly schooled knew that The Occident was a world of spirits in which sages may explore for spiritual things. Nevertheless, old reports alleged that the purple-gowned emperor of the Tachinese hated Persia and if the enigma in the paddies was his far-travelled legate then he may bring good news for The T'ang. So courtiers sacred and profane concurred with The Accomplished One that the stranger must be afforded every civility. Meanwhile, a monk versed in the lore and language of The Occident must hurriedly be procured whilst a lord is caparisoned for treaty. The Court is galvanised. Little do they know that the question is not *whether* Ta-ch'in exists: For it *had* existed, but does not exist, yet is mightier still, and shall conquer in The Sign of Ten[e].

Let Ching-Ching take up the story:-

"When T'ai Tsung, the accomplished Emperor, was beginning his prosperous reign in glory and splendor, with intelligence and wisdom ruling the people, there was in the Kingdom of Ta-ch'in a highly virtuous man called Alopen. He augured from the blue sky and decided to carry the true Sutras with him, and watching the harmony of the winds, he hastened through difficulties and dangers. In the ninth year of Cheng-Kuan he came to Ch'ang-an. The Emperor dispatched Duke Fang Hsuan-ling, his Minister of State, to take an escort to the western suburb to meet the guest and to bring him to the palace".f

So with Confucian diffidence and the tender physiolatry of the Oriental heart the good monk relates the fraught but serene reception.

The barbarian was ushered into The Imperial Presence and thirty damp and dusty codices were discovered in his baggage. Scholars had immense trouble with this intelligence since it was in Syriac, an obscure and uncouth script, and the concepts expounded were neither strategic nor commercial, but very, very strange.

Let "The Book of Praise" explain:-

"Hereby, with great respect, we declare that we examined the list of all the sutras and have found that there are in all 530 sutras belonging to the Religion of Ta-Ch'in. They are, however, all on leave sheets in the Brahmin language. In the ninth year of the Chen-Kuan period in the reign of the Emperor T'ai-tsung of the T'ang, Priest Alopen, Bishop of The Western Lands, arrived in the Middle Kingdom and humbly presented a petition to the Throne in his native tongue.

Fang Hsuan-ling and Wei Ching reverentially submitted the matter to the Imperial Information, when the petition was translated.

Afterwards, by Imperial Orders, the priest Ching-Ching, Bishop of this Religion was summoned and the above thirty mentioned books were translated".

Here is some of what Ching-Ching thought he read:-

"...the brilliant and revered Mi-shih-he, veiling his true majesty, came to earth as a man. An angel proclaimed the good news. A virgin gave birth to the sage in Ta-ch'in. A bright star announced the good news. Persians saw its glory and came to offer gifts. He fulfilled the ancient law of the twenty-four sages, governing the State on the great principle. He founded the new teaching of non-assertion that operates silently through the Holy Spirit of the Three in One and made humanity capable of good works by following the truth. Establishing the standard of the Eight conditions, he purified human nature and perfected truth.

He opened wide the Three constant gates, celebrating life and destroying death. He hung up a brilliant sun to take by storm the halls of darkness. The forces of evil were all defeated. He rowed the boat of mercy and traveled to the palaces of light. In this way were all sentient beings saved. His mighty work completed, he ascended at midday to his original place...
...The true and eternal way is wonderful and yet hard to name. Its benefits and purpose are clearly known and splendid, therefore we name it and call it the Brilliant Teaching."f

The last two sentences are abundantly right in any tongue and reflect the tenets of Chapter One of the Tao Te Ching.
The Imperial Countenance darkened. The audience fell silent. Duke Fang bowed and with tremulous voice asked what he must do with the disheveled foreigner. The Court prostrated as the Emperor rose. Then the wise T'ai Tsung declaimed "Take him to the ambassadorial quarters and afford him every service, holy man or not, as he awaits The Imperial Will". The ladies tittered and hid behind their paper fans as the turning occidental caught their gaze.
T'ai Tsung stalked with sorry steps to the innermost bower of the harem and ordered The Grand Eunuch to remove all from The Presence. Then T'ai Tsung wept, for now he knew, that surrounded by three thousand concubines in the midst of a city of three million souls, he was Alone as no Prince ever had been forlorn; unless it was that weird Tachinese sage who had "hung to take by storm the halls of darkness".
We Europeans have no record of Alopen. We do not even know his Greco-Roman name, if indeed he had such, and not a Semitic one. He must have been one of thousands who vanished into the desert never to be heard of again, like so many of the convicts of Georgian Australia, whose memory survives, if at all, in the lore of aboriginal peoples.
Ching-Ching resumed his work with those difficult texts:-

"The first thing is to obey the Lord of Heaven. The second vow is to act in filial piety and to care for parental needs with true sincerity. All the people who follow the Heaven-Way will make their home there when they die, if they are filial to their father and mother and do not fail to obey what they are told. So we should serve our father and mother for no living thing exists without a mother and father. [lost text]. The fourth vow is that anyone who professes faith in the precepts should thus be kind and good to all living beings and should neither hate anyone, nor harbor evil thoughts about them. The fifth vow is that all people should not only not take life, but should persuade others to do likewise, for the life of all living beings is of equal value to the lives of humans. The sixth vow is that none should commit adultery with another's wife, nor use any persuasion to try to make her commit adultery. The seventh vow is that no one should steal. The eighth vow is that no one should covet another's riches or rank when they see them, nor should they covet his field, house or servants. The ninth vow is that none should plot to bear false witness against another who is happier than he. The tenth vow is that no one should serve the Lord of Heaven with anything that does not belong to that person or at another person's expense.

Beside these there are many other things which you should consider. You should not deceive another person by taking advantage of his defenselessness; if you happen to see a poor child, you should not turn away from him; if your enemy is hungry, you should feed him and give him drink in plenty as well as forgive him and then forget what it was that caused you to make him your enemy. If you happen to see someone having to work very hard, you should assist him and use your own power for his good, as well as give him a drink of milk; if you happen to see another person without clothing, you should give him clothes..."[g]

In 638, T'ai Tsung issued an Imperial Edict of Recognition of the votaries of the Shining Teaching, and his successor Kao Tsung favored the Christians and built Nestorian monasteries in every province whilst the faith spread to every city. Later Hsuan Tsung honored the church, endowing many abbeys, and even inviting priests to hold communion in The Imperial Presence. His successor Su Tsung built four new monasteries and re-established others.

Soon Nestorian Christianity was holding its own beside the other foreign faiths of Buddha and Mohammed.

Nestorius had become a controversial Bishop of Constantinople in the time of Augustine and challenged Orthodoxy with some radical precepts which may commend themselves to the more "rational" theologies of our time:-

1   The Adoptive Character of Christ[h]

"...Jesus was a human being who was 'taken up' by the Spirit of God. This Spirit, known as the Word, bestowed a form of divinity upon Jesus, but that divinity did not affect the fact that he was in essence an ordinary human being like you or me."[1]

2   Mary Christotokos

Mary was not "Mother of God": For God by definition has no primogenitrix. Mary was the bearer of Christ:- "Christotokos".

3   Pelagianism[i]

A very dangerous, but not summarily dismissible, doctrine: In short, the human spirit is intrinsically good, not essentially evil. Hence Original Sin has no theological meaning.

To these Occidental precepts of Nestorian Christianity, the Chinese added extrapolations based upon their own ethico-religious traditions, especially those of Buddhism and the Tao, though strictly-speaking the former is a prior import:-

    4   General Deliverance

The Mercy of Christ extends to all "sentient beings" not just humans, much less Believers only. Accordingly the lives of all animals must be respected and preserved.

    5   Syncretism

Syncretism allowed Chinese Christianity freely to adopt godly teaching from the other faiths with which it came into contact.

When aliens meet the tacitudes are exposed and made explicit as mere conventions, and understanding must be built afresh from its sensual foundations. The result is often an incondite synthesis of sublime and surreal beauty, serenely affective and memorable as no formulaic platitude shared by compatriots could be.

Let The Word tell you of His new-found Chinese Eden, the Mysterious Rest and Joy:-

"It might be compared to a lonely uninhabited mountain, full of all sorts of woods and trees, which have numerous leaves and branches spreading in all directions, giving shade and shelter. Although this mountain and its forests do not invite birds and beasts to come, yet all kinds of birds and beasts will seek this mountain and the forests and will come and settle there, of their own accord."[j]

The Sign of Ten is a cross. The Atonement of The Cross meant little to the Chinese, but the Shining Path of Christ's Brilliant Teaching meant very much to them. Today Christianity has reached the crossroads: The branch it takes shall be its Final Path.

Of our free volition we may reject the wisdom and the faith of foreigners, whether or not they are holding British passports, but only God can decide who or what it is that is thus Consigned to Outer Darkness. Of our free volition we may deny life to those foreigners or other of God's Children, but who or what thereby wins Death Eternal is the Judgment of Another. The Cross has Three Arms but the forest many branches. We may denounce the heathen and the heretic, but only Christ knows all the paths of the forest, for they all lead to His Father. Like latter-day Nehemiahs we can rebuild our walls and exclude the Horonite and the Ammonite but all walls tumble in time for walls like laws are there to be broken.

Martin Palmer is an ecumenical Anglican and environmentalist. I am indebted to him for my knowledge of Alopen and his Chinese Nestorians, and to him for the passages of The Holy Sutras I have quoted. It is therefore fitting that Palmer has the last word:-

"I believe that the Nestorian church in China made a most significant and interesting attempt to translate the gospel, not just into another language, but into another culture and belief system. They were often despised by the nineteenth- and early twentieth-century Protestant missionaries to China. I believe the missionaries were wrong to do so, and that the rejection of the Nestorian's attempts at acculturation perhaps accounts for the fact that despite their efforts - the greatest missionary venture in history - China by 1949 was still less than one per cent Christian.

I believe that the Nestorians can jolt us into seeing how culture-bound our version of the truth of God incarnate in humanity is. They can also challenge us to try and express the gospel in terms of the cultures and beliefs which surround us today, and to do so with integrity but not with dogmatism".[1]

References

1   "Living Christianity"
    Martin Palmer   1993
    Element Books of Shaftesbury
    ISBN 1-85230-327-1

2   "The Nestorian Monument in China"
    PY Saeki   1916
    The Society for the Propagation of Christian Knowledge
    (SPCK)

3   "Nestorian Documents and Relics in China"
    PY Saeki   1937
    The Society for the Propagation of Christian Knowledge
    (SPCK)

Notes

a   The great loess plain of the Wei Valley comprises
    a fertile aeolian silt up to a hundred meters thick.
    This yellow dust is tinted by the hydrous iron
    oxide limonite, the pigment of yellow sand.
    The Wei drains to the Hwang Ho ("Yellow River").

b   An old Cornish word for the brassy crystalline
    mineral iron sulfide or pyrite.
    Pyrite or "fool's gold" often crystallises from black shales
    with which it contrasts both in color and form.

c   The Rome of the East.
    It is probably the case that the identification of
    modern Xian and the fabled Xanadu is defensible
    only upon philological and other circumstantial grounds.
    In any event, the Chinese of The Tang Dynasty called
    their city Ch'ang-an-ch'eng (Walled City of Ch'ang-an).
    Ch'ang-an (meaning "heavenly peace") was founded in 202BC
    near the confluence of the Wei and Ba Rivers and revived
    later by the Sui Emperors.
    In the sixth to seventh centuries AD it was expanded upon a
    hippodamian plan into a central Palace City surrounded by
    an Imperial City for officials and an Outer City suburb
    of artisanal and mercantile premises.

Shortly after at the start of The Tang Dynasty (618-907AD) Xianreached its zenith and the population topped
three million (c.f. Antonine Rome about 1.5 million).
It declined, however, but though Marco Polo reported a thriving trade center, in about 1260AD the
Mongol emperor Kublai Khan moved the capital to Peking.
He continued to use the Wei Valley as an
administrative and supply base.
Modern Xian remains a major spiritual, cultural and industrial center, with temples of many faiths, several general and technical universities, and aircraft, electrical,
chemical and food processing industries.
It is also a major archeological and tourist hub:
Besides its "forest" of religious inscribed stones it has, about twenty miles East, the old Imperial Harem hot springs and the world-famous "terracotta army" burial, together with numerous other world-class monuments.
The 1983 population was 2,180,000.
Scholars identify the Xanadu of Coleridge with
Shang-to or Dolon Nor, both in Inner Mongolia.

d   In 1797 the English poet Samuel Taylor Coleridge (1772-1834) retired sick to stay with friends at Culbone near the Exmoor coast between Lynton and Porlock.
After reading "Purchas's Pilgrimage" and taking an opiate he dozed and on waking hurriedly began to scribble the several hundred lines of verse he had composed about Xanadu.
Unfortunately, he was interrupted by
"a person on business from Porlock"
after jotting a mere fifty-four lines and upon returning indoors realised he had forgotten the rest!
The remnant is the world-famous poem "Kubla Khan".

e   The Chinese numeral for ten is a cross.

f   From the Nestorian Stone at Xian.

g   From the Hsu'ting Mi-shih-he Sutra of 635AD (205 verses).
(The Gospel of Peace of Jesus Christ).

h   I apologise for representing Nestorian doctrine
with a simplistic word.
This tenet should not be confused with the Adoptionist heresies
Of eighth-century Iberia
Palmer is nearer the mark with his summary.

i   Publicised by the British monk Pelagius (fourth century).

j   From the Chih-hsuan-an-lo Sutra.
(The Gospel which attempts Mysterious Rest and Joy).

Catching Creatures

13 February 1999

It is also worth noting that the expression 'Do there exist any so-and-sos?' is often equivalent to '*Are there* any so-and-sos?' Thus '*Are there* any dodos?' means the same as 'Do any dodos *exist*?', while '*Are there* any prime numbers between 25 and 30?' means the same as, 'Do any prime numbers between 25 and 30 *exist*?' Although there is a temptation to assume that 'things which exist' are necessarily *solid* items, standard uses of 'exist' do not justify us in thinking this way. Dodos, when they existed, could properly be described as 'solid' and it would make sense to speak of *capturing* a few - perhaps in a net. However in the case of prime numbers the idea of capturing them or failing to capture them - whether in a net or by any other means - makes no sense. Similarly, if someone were to ask, 'Are there (or do there exist) any duties which are totally overriding?' then, whatever the answer, there is no expectation that, if the answer is 'yes' one might capture some duties in a net. Similarly we may believe that there is a virtue in necessity or that there is safety in numbers without being committed to saying that virtue or safety are 'real entities' - a statement to which it does not seem possible to attach any sense.[1]

Thus with avuncular charm and delicious insolence the psychologist and philosopher Tim Miles casts his gauntlet to whichever theologically-inclined mathematicians may be out there.

In "Speaking of God", Tim asks us, like latter-day Corinthians, to put childish things aside and repudiate "Magnus", the autonomous sentience of tutelary Immanence as we move to a more adult appreciation of Godhead, the Essence of our own best Aspirations. My contention is that Tim's analysis is deeply flawed, but it is very gladly that I receive the gift of his richly-considered Testimony, which wrought with scholarship and humor, is a milestone contribution to Postmodern theology and the evolving Quaker debate on doctrine.

Since 1931 even mathematicians have had to accept that certitude is not of earthly life and whilst I can adduce no Proofs it may be that if there can be Virtue even in Necessity then I can demonstrate that there is no Safety in Numbers, whether very little numbers, such as some Societies muster, or very big numbers, as some Churches boast. For whilst rectitude eludes the individual, the error of the multitude is unanimous.

The epigraph gives you an inkling of "Speaking of God"'s conceptual density, adumbrating primality, existence, network, plenum and void in a mere 228 words. These concepts of primality, existence, network, plenum and void are so inextricably intermeshed that it would take another Euclid[a] to abstract the axioms and build a systematic elaboration.

But before we may address these fascinating issues we must first discuss nothing, and in particular nothing at all.

One day in 1973 an undergraduate geologist doodled on his notepad as he awaited the arrival of a friend in The Leamington Rooms[b]. Euclid said that a point is that with no part and a line that which has extension without breadth. The student quickly determined that the most primitive zero-dimensional object has one vertex (point); the basic one-dimensional figure has two vertices and an edge (line); the fundamental two-dimensional object, three edges, three vertices, and one surface (triangle); and finally the basic three-dimensional solid, the tetrahedron, has four vertices, six edges, four faces and one volume.

Clearly these counts are the coefficients of polynomial expansions of $(x+1)^{d+1}$ where x is arbitrary and d the object's dimensionality, so that the indices of x denote the dimensionality of the component form.

For example, for the line:-

$$(x+1)^{1+1} = 1x^2 + 2x^1 + x^0$$

Equation One

and for the tetrahedron:-

$$(x+1)^{3+1} = 1x^4 + 4x^3 + 6x^2 + 4x^1 + x^0$$

Equation Two

whilst by extrapolation the basic four-dimensional polytop sports five contained volumes, and ten faces with ten edges meeting at five points on its "periphery".

These expansions generate the Pascal triangle beloved of statisticians, but our interest centers upon that ever-present lowest-degree term whose coefficient is always unity and which characterises every dimension for it represents the very principle of geometrical nullity: The Void which inheres everywhere.

Even the poor old point, standing partless and apparently naked, marking position without inclusion, has his invisible partner standing forever at his side like some binary twin whose presence is betrayed only by subtle and eccentric nutations.

It is important to realise that x^0 is the "marker" of The Void, in some sense *descriptive* of nullity. Mathematically it is of course one so it is certainly not zero, which cipher is a recent concept, possibly of Indian origin, and at any rate unknown to The (European) Ancients. However, our Ancients certainly understood The Void and declared that "Nature abhors a vacuum", a view to which medieval Aristotelians assented, until Evangelista Torricelli began to develop its physical reality. Indeed, so far as such interpretations *can* make sense, it seems that Democritus and his Epicurean followers at Rome conceived of particles entirely filling available space even if this had to imply a crystalline ether in the superlunary wastes, a concept not wholly abandoned until the days of Relativity.

Dalton resurrected Democritus and particulate nature filled every interstice of the plenum until the probings of Wilson and Rutherford and the paradigms of Einstein corroded the concept of the solid. We now know that almost the entire volume of any atom is void: That its curtilage is patrolled by tiniest motes of matter, epicene in their indecision over whether they are bodily stuff or smeared energy: That the nucleus is composite: That the baryons of the nucleus are composite and that Absolute Nothingness is not just ubiquitous, but immanent.

So why shout "liar!" when John tells us that The Risen Christ walked through walls and locked doors, or Luke that He ate broiled fish and honeycomb, or vanished from the table at Emmaus?

Why balk at Resurrection when Christ Himself was casual to insouciance about the performance of what is clearly a technical procedure, whether by Himself or others? And The Ancients treat it as a common trick amongst both pagan holy men and secular physicians?

Tim makes much of both "the supernatural" and of the Post-Renaissance emergence of "the supernatural" as a concept to discredit "Magnus thinking" but he correctly notes that the idea was alien to The Ancients and the words "supernatural" and "non-material" are absent from The Bible. For clearly "the supernatural" is only the "unexplained" as that not assimilated to human understanding and accordingly "natural" or "scientific". Men who believe that a luminosity above a grave is the spirit of the departed or "Will of the Wisp" have not heard of fools' fire from the burning of methane, the same phenomenon as takes place in any modern gas-fired kitchen.

Never mind The Answer: What is the question?

Tim makes much of "facts" and their influence on "Magnus thinking" but numbers do not exist in the realm of "solid items" and questions about the existence of dodos are qualitatively different and utterly incomparable with number theoretic statements. Existence itself is of several different species and if God created the dodo then man created the count.

Post-Classical European Science is based upon Mathematics, the art of systematic generalisation. Normal people call the selection and articulation of generalisations opinion. Ergo Science is opinion. So far so Postmodern. But the fallibility of opinion cannot be used to disprove the creation or its contained creatures, for opinion itself is created. So what argument may be adduced to talk the Creator out of His Scheme, whether or not the Creator engendered The Universe in any materialistic sense?

We do not have to capture Categorical Imperatives in a net, for duties are defined by description not selection, as are Virtue and Safety.

If Resurrection is a reality then "when they existed" is a specious qualifier of dodos, for they persist, or shall regenerate, and maintain their arrestability and their elusoriness as ever they did.

The point of this argument is that when we speak of "solid" items of the kind we can capture "in a net" we have to remember that solidity is highly qualified, and to argue that only the "solid" can "exist" is not necessarily materialist. Conversely, it is neither an argument for nor against "Magnus": the primitive omnipotent personal godhead satirised by Tim in his provocative little book.

There is another conception of nullity which is neither zero nor any reification, physical or metaphysical, of The Void. It is something known to mathematicians as The Empty Set $\emptyset$. It can be imagined as a container with infinitely-thin glass walls and inside it is Literally None of the category of objects under discussion. If the category under discussion is "Life, The Universe and Everything" then The Empty Set, the contents of your magic glass box, is Literally Nothing At All. Note that this is *not* 0 (zero)^c and it is not x^0 (the void): It is $\emptyset$ (nothing at all). For example, consider the set of counting integers n=0,1,2,3,4,5,....,1067,1068,....,∞. (This species of ∞ [infinity] is called $\aleph_0$ [aleph null], for a description of which see below). If a set contains 1, 6 and 7 it is clearly not empty if you are discussing a set of integers. And if it contains 0 and zero only it *is not empty* and is not The Empty Set $\emptyset$.

This implies that there are at least three different conceptions of nullity:-

    (a)   Denotative

This attaches a purely *nominal* label to nullity, i.e. 0 (zero), which is a purely practical convenience but enormously dangerous because careless people confuse it with "the real thing".

    (b)   Descriptive

Description tries to *define* the subject implicitly by elaborating some or all of its *properties*. Set theory is a simple scheme of description which treats of association. The Empty Set ∅ attempts to describe pure non-association in terms of the wholly absent *constituting* nothing at all.

    (c)   Ipsitive

This is not symbolism but "the real thing" standing there before your face being itself. It has no need of names and no arts of description, whether scientific, graphic, plastic, literary or prophetic, can make it more or less real. Even x^0 is only a symbol, at some level both Unity and Vacancy, and even this only intimates a starker reality.

The Ancients were very familiar with certain technologies which are obscure to us, or even forgotten. It is only in the last ninety years that informatic exigencies in the pressure of war have renewed human interest in the character of some things Ancients took for granted: The Filter and The Net.

The idea of capturing primes in a net makes eminent sense for that is how our father of primes, Eratosthenes[d] first caught them.

Figure One illustrates the principle of The Sieve of Eratosthenes[2]. If we stop (merely for convenience) at a maximum tested integer of twenty-five we can use The Sieve to filter out all the primes between 1 and 25 by excluding all multiples of the numbers between 2 and 5. Those four series of multiples are, if you will, four stacked nets of *increasing* mesh size.

Nets and Filters are not always made of nylon, paper or gallium arsenide. Indeed the old thermionic valves that De Forest would have recognised were almost all vacuum ("the void", "nothing at all").

We have spoken of nets of the flesh and the mind. Perhaps it was a net of the spirit that The Preacher had in mind when he said:-

For man also knoweth not his time: as the fishes that are taken in an evil net, and as the birds that are caught in the snare; so are the sons of men snared in an evil time, when it falleth suddenly upon them.[e]

The Sieve of Eratosthenes

```
Integers into    →  1 2 3 4 5 6 7 8 9 10 11 12 13 14 15 16 17 18 19 20 21 22 23 24
The Sieve

Multiples of 2   →        4   6   8  10    12    14    16    18    20    22    24
Multiples of 3   →            6      9     12       15       18       21       24
Multiples of 4   →                8          12       16          20          24
Multiples of 5   →                      10          15             20

Primes Collect   →  1 2 3   5   7       11    13          17    19          23
Here
```

Figure One

Tim asks "Do any prime numbers between 25 and 30 exist?". I should explain to non-mathematicians that a prime number is a whole number that is only *integrally* divisible by itself and unity. Thus as above 1,3,5,7,11,13,17,19 and 23 are all prime, but so, uniquely for an even number, is 2. The primes are a subset of the set of counting integers, {n}. Why? Because we say so. To me, Tim failed to ask the really interesting question "Do any prime numbers between 14 and 16 exist?".

You see, the answer devolves about primacy in more ways than the obvious, because all our knowledge of prime numbers is of a second-level descriptive character: We cannot just call them "primes" and leave it nominally at that, for labels are only of value when the objects to which they adhere are manifest. On the other hand, we cannot behold the naked splendor of the *res* itself, since primes are neither corporeal or spiritual, being (as Kronecker would have had it) "works of man". You may as well call "Jim Warren" any convenient name such as "Florence" or "The Luguvalian" since all such appellations are only of interest in distinguishing the entity from similars whilst description is superfluous save for clinical or identificatory purposes.

Now we Europeans see Eratosthenes, Euclid and even Fermat[f] as the pioneers of primes. With typical oracularity Euclid *declared* the prime to be "that which is measured by the unit alone", but the Chinese[3] had priority over Eratosthenes by two hundred years when they *defined* the odd prime, p, using:-

$$w = \frac{2^{p-1} - 1}{p}$$

Equation Three

where w=1,2,3,...,$\aleph_0$; any whole number.

The Chinese thought that they had defined the prime in the vulgar Western sense but what they had *actually* defined was a more general class of pseudoprimes, more plentiful than the primes, and yet also of infinite abundance.

For Cantor proved that just as nothingness comes in several different sorts so does boundlessness. $\aleph_0$ (Aleph Null) is what you or I call ∞ (infinity), denumerable with matches to each natural number. $\aleph_1$ is also infinite but yet denser and "more" than $\aleph_0$ since it is the count of the functions of completed infinity.

Now Euclid proved the infinity of the primes, and yet since primes are clearly sparser and "fewer" than the counting numbers they boast an inferior sort of infinitude.

Mercy is a sub-category of Love, so the natural theological implication is that whilst The Love of Christ is limitless yet it is more than what we could ever cope with. Therefore Christ offers instead his Mercy which is "less" than Love but equally infinite.

In fact it was AD1819 until the prior Chinese definition was *invalidated by accepted Greco-Roman criteria* when it was discovered that $2^{340} - 1$ was exactly divisible by 341 (a European composite: 341=11×31) that is the first known pseudoprime. Since that discovery the Chinese Conjecture has been generalised to:-

$$w = \frac{n^{p-1} - 1}{p}$$

Equation Four

and whole swarms of new pseudoprimes have emerged from the interstices of the natural numbers, including 9,15,91,124 and others, numbers normally indubitably composite.

That which is crooked cannot be made straight: and that which is wanting cannot be numbered.^g

But Ecclesiastes was clearly no geometer and less an arithmetician!

Tim gave us "Magnus": the personal Almighty Father of Old Testament Creation and Magnus has spent three thousand years inculcating crude and even materialistic "Magnus thinking". Tim contrasts this with a gender-neutral, thoroughly Postmodern, genius of collective consciousness "beyond theism and atheism", finite in time and collateral with, if not generated by, the human will. Tim does not dignify this latter creature with an appellation but for common convenience I christen him "Albertus" because I seem to remember from my boyhood reading of chemistry that Albertus Magnus discovered antinomy (or was it arsenic?).

But Tim's discrimination of these two godheads depends upon a valid distinction of Realism and Idealism and the implicit thesis that they are mutually-preclusive philosophies. My argument is that Albertus-Magnus is a non-concept which arises from a mistaken (but very sophisticated) vision of either/or logico-ideological exclusion. I am at pains to reassure hurried readers that my emphasis upon culture, history and the definitional integrity of primes elaborated above does *not* reinforce the Postmodern manifesto of relativism and projection. It merely illustrates the way in which unknowables are cataphatically described by human thinkers. Such descriptions are for ever incomplete, erroneous, special or even self-referent, but this cannot prejudice the ipsitive reality of the *res* which such descriptions reflect. I am, if you will, proposing an inverse Platonic Cave in which the Forms mirror the Substance they shadow.

I think you agree that Tim and Jim have said enough for now. So let John have the Last Word:-

Simon Peter saith unto them, I go fishing. They say unto him, We also go with thee. They went forth, and entered into a ship immediately; and that night they caught nothing. But when the morning was now come, Jesus stood on the shore: but the disciples knew not that it was Jesus. Then Jesus saith unto them, Children, have ye any meat? They answered him, No. And he said unto them, Cast the net on the right side of the ship, and ye shall find. They cast therefore, and now they were not able to draw it for the multitude of fishes. Therefore that disciple whom Jesus loved saith unto Peter, It is the Lord. Now when Simon Peter heard that it was the Lord, he girt his fisher's coat unto him, (for he was naked,) and did cast himself into the sea. And the other disciples came in a little ship; (for they were not far from land, but as it were two hundred cubits,) dragging the net with fishes. As soon as they were come to land, they saw a fire of coals there, and fish laid thereon, and bread. Jesus saith unto them, Bring of the fish which ye have now caught. Simon Peter went up, and drew the net to land full of great fishes, an hundred and fifty and three[h]: and for all there were so many, yet was not the net broken. Jesus saith unto them, Come and dine. And none of the disciples durst ask him, Who art thou? knowing that it was the Lord. Jesus then cometh, and taketh bread, and giveth them, and fish likewise. This is now the third time that Jesus shewed himself to his disciples, after that he was risen from the dead.[i]

Acknowledgments

I am very grateful to Jane Mitchell, Robert Organ and Alex Tindall, all of Tarbert Meeting, for proposing several improvements to the manuscript.

References

1. "Speaking of God"
   TR Miles 1998
   William Sessions Limited of York
   ISBN 1-85072-202-1
   pp 111
   (The epigraph is Paragraph 3: Page 21)

2. "Numbers, Their History and Meaning"
   Graham Flegg 1983
   Pelican Series
   Penguin Books of Harmondsworth
   ISBN 0-14-02.2564-1

3. "Think of a Number"
   Malcolm E Lines 1990
   Institute of Physics Publishing of Bristol
   ISBN 0-85274-183-9
   pp 163
   (Pages 67 and 68)

4. "History of Mathematics"
   David Eugene Smith 1923
   Volumes I and II
   Dover Publications Incorporated of New York
   ISBN 0-486-20429-4

5. The Mathematical Gazette
   V82:N495   November 1998
   ISSN 0025-5572
   (Page 378)

Notes

a   Euclid of Alexandria (born c365BC)
compiled the thirteen books of The Elements,
an exhaustive compendium of early Hellenistic
mathematics, and the basis of numerical science
until the 1820's AD.

b   The basement of The Faculty of Arts Building at
The Victoria University of Manchester, England.

c   Confusion over notation persists, whether unconsciously
or with specialist intention.
Computerists (including I) usually write zero as $\varnothing$
which can even be confounded with "cancelled naught"
as illustrated in the elegant Proof of Divine Beatitude
with which "Theologian" further enlivened the already
uproarious pages of the latest Mathematical Gazette[5]:-

$$GO\varnothing Dx \frac{1}{\varnothing} = GOD$$

$$\therefore God\ is\ infinite\ good$$

d   Eratosthenes (276-198BC), (post-Euclid)
mathematician and poet, was educated at Athens and taught at
Alexandria University where he was librarian.
He computed the circumference and diameter of the Earth
by comparing the noontide zeniths of the Sun at
Syene (Aswan) and Alexandria, towns known to be separated
by 5000 stadia of longitude.
Since the zeniths differed by 7°12' it followed that the
circumference of the planet was 250000 stadia or
24465.8 miles or 40030 kilometers, an error of 1.7%.
Plutarch reports that Eratosthenes gave the range of the Sun
as 804 million stadia and the Moon 780 thousand.
At a rate of 10.218356 stadia to the mile the respective errors
are 18% (less at perihelion) and 313%.[4]

e   Ecclesiastes 9:12

f   Pierre de Fermat (1608-1665),
French jurist and mathematician, a student of Diophantus and the author of several great and fecund conjectures in number theory.

g   Ecclesiastes 1:15

h   153 is pregnant both with number theoretic and numerological "meaning" based upon operations involving three and has obvious Trinitarian implications.
It is the seventeenth triangular number.

i   John 21:3;14

Sin

24 October 2008

Sin is any cruelty that you inflict. It is not necessarily malicious or consciously intended. Sin always has a living victim, and it hurts or harms your victim. God qualifies as a living victim. So, potentially, do you.

You are not born sinful: Only with the capacity to sin.

In this discussion of sin I shall say little of evil people who act with malice, or people who commit serious statute crimes. They need pastoral support for sure, and some would benefit from confessional penance. But they have complex needs and require the care of medical and penal specialists.

You are a good person and your needs differ.

Over and above human conceptions of sin are the imperative Commandments of God that were handed down to Moses as he wondered through the desert. They are listed in Chapter Twenty of Exodus and again in Deuteronomy 5:1-21. Adapting the Commandments of God for the rich young man (Matthew 19:16-22) Our Holy Savior said: "Do not kill", "Do not steal", "Do not commit adultery", "Do not bear false witness", "Love thy neighbor", and "Honor your Father and Mother".

Using modern language these Ten Commandments of God are in order:-

1. Have No Other Gods
2. Make No Idols
3. Do Not Take God's Name in Vain
4. Keep the Sabbath Holy
5. Honor Your Father and Mother
6. Do Not Kill
7. Do Not Commit Adultery
8. Do Not Steal
9. Do Not Lie to Get Someone into Trouble
10. Do Not Be Jealous

If these articles are obeyed men live like angels. To our lasting cost many disobey each by habit and all break some on occasion.

To disobey the Injunctions of Christ or any Commandment of God is a Mortal Sin. It is a very serious matter that is always hurtful. You have noticed something else about Mortal Sins: They usually involve concealment or some other act of cowardice.

In an attempt to be helpful, Pope Gregory I compiled a list of Seven Deadly Sins which are also confessable.

Here is a list of Pope Gregory's sins or vices with their corresponding virtues:-

Sin	Virtue
Lust	Chastity
Gluttony	Temperance
Greed	Charity
Sloth	Diligence
Wrath	Patience
Envy	Kindness
Pride	Humility

Gregory's list is only a guide. You will know if you have sinned, and if you need a technical diagnosis a little meditation may yield it. Gregory's sins tend to divide into sins of the mind (Pride, Envy and Wrath) and sins of the flesh (Sloth, Greed, Gluttony and Lust). But of course these evils overlap and interpenetrate. A problem with the Deadly Sins is that they are not actions but thoughts that promote action, and thoughts are not sinful of themselves. On the other hand they are a useful list of tendencies to be suppressed.

Sins are formulated in your mind, or arise from a culpable absence of care. Carelessness and indolence are sins of Sloth. You cannot blame Satan or anyone else for your own shortcomings. Satan, too, is a helpless bystander, utterly reliant upon your exercise of Free Will.

It is possible to sin against God though the normal layman can only do so in the one way. God's Third Commandment says you should not take His name in vain. This means you do not call his name unless you truly want him to listen and to help you become the person He wants you to be, or to help some creature you find it hard to help yourself. You do not call him as a matter of ceremony, to progress some kind of administrative procedure, or to impress your friends. You certainly do not do so by stupid habit. Swearing on the Bible in a court of law is blasphemy. The court is the court of your king, not of God. Render unto God the things that are of God, and unto Caesar the things that are Caesar's (Matthew 22:21).

If you call out the Name of God without expecting him to respond you are as much a coward as if you unwarrantably called out for your king or president, whilst being safely out of earshot. Real men and real women do not swear.

The antithesis of swearing is prayer. When you pray you sincerely want God to hear and to act. You are ready to face him. You know that if you abuse the call you could be punished most grievously, unless He is merciful, though He has proven himself to be so. Prayer is for real men and women.

When I was an atheist swearing had no effect on me. Probably I did not notice most of it. If I swore I thought nothing of it. When I swear now, and I just did, I know I am a disgusting coward and hypocrite. Every time I hear the words it is like a whiplash upon my soul.

Blasphemy defiles a man, as prayer sounds sweet upon the lips of a woman and a curse of complaint unfruitful.

Minced oaths are just extra craven ones, as they imply that whilst we have dismissed the appearance of God as too improbable to fear, yet we live in terror of the censure of men. These include the British swearword "bl**dy", the one that crossed my lips, and the vocative expression "for f**k's sake", that traduces not only the Divine itself but also a sacred act appointed of it.

Please do not swear.

It is possible to sin against yourself, but whilst the sin may cause you pain, it is your loved ones who suffer. Lust, Gluttony and Sloth are sins against the self. Who pays when you indulge yourself? Think about it.

Pride is the source of many of the sins and real crimes committed by men and women who try to do good.

Three weeks ago my new neighbor moved in. His new house had been unoccupied for nearly a year and a summer's growth luxuriated his garden and the Leylandii hedge that bounded it. Proudly and industriously he trimmed these high untidy hedges and he made a very good job of so doing. He and his were very happy to enter their new home. I wonder if he spared a thought for the tiny creatures who lost theirs. Disconsolate little birds spent the day fluttering through my shrubbery, distressing themselves and their neighbors. Would you like your home destroyed? Pride had led to cruelty.

A few days later I passed an angler beside a canal. He was torturing small fish. He was about forty years old and if you are foreign you possibly wonder that a grown man would, but I digress. He accosted me to ask that I take pictures of him and then revealed a magnificent dying pike from a keep net. I asked him if he was going to eat it but he said he would place it back in the canal. He posed with the fish but was dissatisfied with my captures. Cruelty had led to Pride and then to Wrath.

The gentle snails *Helix Aspersa* love my garden (or is it their garden?), and when it rains come out to graze. When I open gates or pace the tarmac I often forget to look out for them. Proudly I prefer my thoughts. I crush the life from them, violating the Sixth Commandment of God. This is a Mortal Sin arising from Pride and nothing less avuncular than my Deadly Sin of Sloth.

Real men do not kill. Real men pass their Sacred Seed of Life to a woman. Real women bear the new life of which they were Entrusted, and nurture it.

Please do not kill.

Almost everyone named in the following narrative was a Christian man or woman who attended Confession regularly according to his rite. Most of them were highly principled. There is one exception. And that exception was a man of the highest judgment and probity.

One day, not so long ago, but in a fairytale country, thirty-year-old Rudolf and his seventeen-year-old mistress Marie were having dinner in their remote hunting lodge. Rudolf's father told him to leave Marie, but Rudolf broke the Fifth Commandment. It was a bleak and snowy January night outside. The furniture was Spartan but the food lavish and Rudolf ordered another bottle of his favorite champagne. Perhaps it is harsh to judge Marie, but Rudolf had also broken the Seventh Commandment, and knew it. Very surprisingly, for the roads were almost snowbound, a deputation arrived. No one knows what happened next but when Rudolf and his lover were found their corpses betrayed signs of extreme violence and at least Rudolf had taken a bullet. Someone had suffered Wrath and broken the Sixth Commandment.

Rudolf's inheritance passed to his fifty-six year old uncle Karl who quickly demurred and passed the poisoned chalice to his twenty-five-year old son, Franz Ferdinand.

Ten years passed.

Franz Ferdinand went to see his aging uncle, Franz Josef. Ferdinand, now in his late thirties, had some very good news. He had proposed marriage to the love of his life, Sophie, and she had accepted. Ferdinand asked his uncle Josef for permission to marry, for although he was of age, custom demanded such.

Franz Josef filled with wrath. He told his nephew that permission was refused on the grounds that Sophie was a Czech and a mere aristocrat. Racism and snobbery are evils borne of Pride, and have very strange and unlooked-for results, as we shall discover. Franz Josef had forgotten that his sacred duty to love his country and his class must not be adulterated with hate for any. Secondly, Josef told Ferdinand that if he married Sophie he and his heirs would be disinherited. Thirdly, and perhaps most cruelly, Josef specified that henceforth Ferdinand and Sophie should never be seen together in public, except on military business.

Ferdinand exercised his human right freely to chose and marry his life partner, and beget her children. Ferdinand and Sophie wed.

On 28th June 1900, Franz Ferdinand swore a morganatic oath that deprived he and his heirs of the throne of Austria forever. Ferdinand broke the Third Commandment. He also disobeyed Christ's Injunction about hair color.

Franz Ferdinand decided to spend the fourteenth anniversary of his oath inspecting his uncle's army in Bosnia. He appeared to regard the day as a kind of commemoration, perhaps of his liberation to married bliss and fatherhood. It meant he could be far from Vienna and with his beloved, out and around the sunlit streets of Sarajevo. Old photographs show the couple beaming nervously but delightedly to well-wishers and shaking hands, she with her bouquet of red roses, he in his army uniform.

June 28th, St Vitus Day, dawned hot and dusty. On that day five hundred and twenty-five years previously a Serb had killed the Sultan of Turkey. It was a national holiday. Gavrilo loved his country and his woman above life itself. Gavrilo was nineteen. Gavrilo slipped his FN1910 9mm semi-automatic into his pocket. He went out to meet his friends.

Ferdinand and Sophie went to Mass. They took the brief train ride to the Bosnian capital and alighted. They climbed into their green Gräf und Stift Rois de Blougnie open tourer to be driven about their duties.

The Appel Quay is a leafy lungotevere beside the River Miljacka. At ten that morning, the couple left the barracks and drove along the Appel Quay to The Town Hall, where Ferdinand would recite his prepared speech. In the garden of the Mostar Cafe Mehmed waited to kill them. He chickened-out. Further on, Vaso, too, had a bomb and a gun. He too chickened-out.

At 1010 the royal car approached Nedeljko. He threw a grenade. The driver put his foot down, and the bomb bounced from Ferdinand's car, and did not explode until a following aides' car was above it. Twenty were injured. Nedeljko chewed his cyanide pill, but it failed to kill him. So he jumped into the Miljacka which proved to be four inches deep. He was arrested. Ferdinand and Sophie continued to the Town Hall. Their car sped quickly and Gavrilo and his group failed to act.

At the Town Hall, Mayor Curcic made a speech of welcome. Ferdinand succumbed to anger and protested his violent reception to his luckless host. Sophie told her husband to be quiet. Presently, Franz Ferdinand's bloodstained script arrived and he recited its ironic thanks.

After this reception Sophie and Ferdinand abandoned their schedules. At 1045 they climbed back into the Gräf und Stift to drive to visit the injured in hospital.

Meanwhile a disappointed Gavrilo had consoled himself with a sandwich and possibly a stiff drink in Schiller's Cafe on a corner at the Quay. In the confusion the Franz Ferdinand motorcade separated. Ferdinand's driver, Leopold, reversed to rejoin the convoy. The backing car paused before Schiller's.

For a suspended moment all that could be heard in the shimmering morning heat was the soft susurration of the gathering foehn in the overhead wires, the clatter of the tappets and the gentle muffled phut of the exhaust.

In this interval, Gavrilo was astounded to recognise his intended victims. Gavrilo stepped from the shadows. He draw his FN1910 and shot Ferdinand through the jugular. Firing again, he punctured Sophie's abdomen. The woman turned and fell on her knees before her bleeding husband with a prayer on her lips.

Gavrilo had forgotten his sacred duty to love without hate and to reverence the world and its creatures.

Franz Ferdinand died saying "Sophie, Sophie, don't die. Live for our children. My pain, it is nothing". Anton, a Jesuit priest, gave him his Last Rites. Sophie died ten minutes later.

The conspirators were arrested. The Austrian Police confiscated Gavrilo's weapon. The Belgian maker's mark disclosed that it was the property of Serbian Military Intelligence. But in any case, the conspirators had readily divulged their complicity with The Serbian Government.

Gavrilo was tried for high treason, but the Austrians did not hang him, for he was adjudged too young. He got twenty years..

So did Nedeljko. He apologised for the grenade attack at the Quay. Ferdinand and Sophie's three young orphans, Sophie, Maximilian and Ernst, decided to exercise their sacred duty to love without hate. They wrote Nedeljko a letter of forgiveness for his attempt on their parents' lives. All three of Ferdinand and Sophie's children would spend World War Two in Dachau concentration camp.

Austria sent Serbia an ultimatum. If satisfied in full, Serbian independence would effectively extinguish. Serbia quibbled.

Austria mobilised its army as if to occupy the proud little Balkan state. Russia guaranteed Serbian independence and mobilised against Austria. Germany was obliged by treaty to defend Austria from any threat. Germany mobilised. Furthermore, Russia and France had secretly guaranteed Serbia at the inception of the statelet some forty years before. And France in turn guaranteed Russia, as was reciprocated.

When governments start guaranteeing things you know you are in trouble.

Now Germany's priority, as always, was to knock France out of a war and fight, if at all, on a single front. But the hills of the Vosges separate the two countries, and are a tough terrain. You do not want your troops beleaguered. The coastal plains of Flanders are a much softer and faster route to France.

Britain had guaranteed Belgian independence at the inception of the Belgian state in 1830. The Germans crossed Belgium. The British declared war.

Soon a continent was in flames and a civilisation tottered. A fifty-year hemoclysm had commenced. In this first phase of it ten million died and 7.6 million disappeared without trace. Europe's race of horses was virtually exterminated and replaced with petrol engines. The Russians could not stand their losses. They called 47-year-old lawyer Vladimir from exile and he tried to take charge.

Russian emperor Nicholas asked his cousin George for shelter. He begged that at least his wife and children might have sanctuary. George promised rescue.

George was next in trouble. His country was resourceful but ill-led. Socialists were restive, feminists were burning property, and the Irish rose in open revolt. George felt his crown slipping. George reneged.

The Russians arrested their emperor Nicholas and his wife Alix, and, together with their five young children, and their loyal staff, murdered them. The Russians continued to fight each other. Five million died.

Germany was defeated and humiliated. In wrath a whole nation sought vengeance, and another fifty-five million died across a planet, thirteen million murdered in cold blood.

In the pages of his Inferno the poet Dante Alighieri had Satan take a man's love and turn it into a travesty of itself.

Franz Josef was a damaged man who loved.

All of the men we named were good men. They loved and lost. They loved the people around them and sought their happiness.

But they forgot The Will of God. They thought their ideas were best, and that honor, loyalty and intellect would suffice. They forgot their enemies were men, and also sought love. They forgot that their children must breed, and that the father is not the child. We shall remember them.

Why?

18 April 1999

The British attack on Serbia is the most dangerous and most unreasonable event of my lifetime. One is compellingly reminded of that other decadent monarchy which wagered its rash grandiloquence in the shadow of a power. But Austria's assault had an obvious, if specious, pretext, and was preceded by an executable list of demands, however humiliating those imperatives were.

I usually write to clarify my own thoughts to myself rather than for less selfish reasons. I try to understand the Meaning of Christ's Message in a modern World. But today, Friends, I offer you nothing, because I do not even *think* I understand the issues involved.

What is the rôle, if any, of these factors:-

(a) The need for Systems Testing to identify organisational and technical shortcomings before a planned general conflict (as in pre-war Spain).

(b) The need for Systems Testing and Publicity for purely commercial objectives, (c.f. The Falklands).

(c) The alleged operation of The Lotka-Volterra Dynamic and other "purely" scientific effects governing competition and predation between species and intraspecific populations.

(d) The need of the Present Government(s) to secure Electoral Return after lackluster (and very "unsocialist") incumbencies.

(e) Tony Blair's Personal Interpretation of Christian Witness.

(f) The Friends' Peace Testimony today.

(g) The "need" to "cleanse" Europe of Islam.

Please assist this newcomer to understand this conflict and what a Quaker should do to ameliorate it.

Eclipse in Mexico

9 September 1999

He hath shewed thee, O man, what is good; and what doth the LORD require of thee, but to do justly, and to love mercy, and to walk humbly with thy God?[1]

Thus with tender heart and awful portent yet another obscure Iron Age tribesman shouts his counsel down the centuries to a bewildered posterity.

My happiest hours were spent walking with my Heavenly Father. Not since my most childish years when I toddled in delighted trust beside my earthly daddy have I felt the perfusing balm of undemanding and unconditional love beside the all wise and unknowable, and felt the guiding hand of unjustified concern. This I know for I have felt.

How well I know mercy for I have often been its heir as friends have rescued me and enemies redeemed me from my own follies at the risk of their livelihoods. Or watched hands of piety or skill remit my pain and that of others in a thousand clement acts of will. This I know for I have seen.

But what is just? I take the words of Micah very seriously. Not because I view his fulfilled prophesies as some vulgar guarantee of the rest of his authority, but because I wonder what he really asks and whether he *entirely* understood the Will of God. Justice perplexes me: I have never seen justice applied, have never received justice, nor dispensed it, nor even seen it given to others. Even the jurists, who have spent lifetimes on its evolution, have not defined it. They seem, as Shakespeare did of mercy, to assume it God-given, a simple and inscrutable axiom which sort of rains down from clear sky to the forges of the forum.

Is justice a kind of vanity, a satanic chimera sent with honor to cultivate the *superbia* of he who called himself Homo *Sapiens*? For sure, we know Vengeance, for who has not said "it serves him right" when his enemy has suffered as he wished to see? And we know Equity for we said "that seems fair" when our friend received a generous legacy from the uncle she nursed in his final years. And most of all we know Policy, for we know that crime must be punished to encourage the others and control those who may disrupt.

But we do not know justice and fear that we may have to concur with St John the Divine and the old-time calvinists who saw it as the perfect and inscrutable Will of God, revealed in Judgment, beyond human preparation and therefore beyond human control.

Lord Justice Scarman is a humane man of some little experience upon the bench. In 1981 there was unrest in England and many black men said they had been tortured by white police whilst in secret custody. Scarman proposed a cadre of "lay visitors", independent citizens empowered to inspect police cells and interview police prisoners by surprise at the time of the visitor's choosing. I am such a Lay Visitor. The local policemen have tedious and frequently sordid duties not relieved by existential paradox or intellectual discussions with cultured clients or learned counsel. Yet they impress with a nearly consistent tenor of matter-of-fact equanimity and brisk courtesy improved at one station by a cheerful *esprit-de-corps* and lively humor in the dingy basement where they must work. The criminals their clients are not exactly brutalised monsters either. They are mostly unintelligent and often opiated young men whose aspiration seems to devolve about cigarettes: Their source, availability and means of ignition. This is Policy in action: Everyone knows the rules and what happens next and banal questions are asked and answered and it is Christian names only in a tacit economy of mutual dependence. Reader, is this justice? Are its postcedents in the courtroom justice or their sequel in the prison?

I live in a conservative European monarchy that preserves the full panoply of kingly dominion. Whether we like it or not, military things dominate our society and our culture. The Army is very valuable to our highest and lowest classes and we have an impossibly high kind of officer called a Brigadier General. Now I am no expert, but it seems to me that all Brigadier Generals are Knights of the Realm. Legend has it that they have no ordinary duties, but patrol the London parks on gray steeds splendid in full uniform as they receive the obeisances of passers-by. They are the butt of many old English jokes, few suited to rehearsal in a devotional magazine. Their substantive function is the representation of British military intent in front of ambassadors and other exulted foreigners, work for which their execrable French and incomprehensible accents fit them perfectly. Notwithstanding the above, I should say that it was well within the occupational competency of a Brigadier General to agitate for the welfare of private soldiers. Some of them would, doubtless, regard such as a God-given privilege were it to become necessary. But I know well enough that such a mission would be the most perilous that such an officer could ever assume.

I teach in a technical college and this is Enrolment Week. Last Tuesday night a father brought his son to enrol on a GNVQ two-year full-time course, which is an elementary commercial qualification for "non-academic" teenagers. The young man looked like a very tiny child to me and in my foolish way I turned to his father and asked his age. "Sixteen". I thought back to my days as a sixteen-year-old who had left school early with little and rudderless. I told the young man to forget GNVQ; to concentrate on the computing which he loved though colleagues elsewhere had rejected him for the appropriate course; to win a nest of good GCSEs; and re-consider his future in two years time from a position of strength. What was more, I said, do not do the GCSEs at my college; try a better one instead. I do not know what the shy and nervous young applicant made of all this but his father was not well-pleased though he forced a simper as we shook hands and parted. I may have shown mercy but did I do justly? My colleagues, many of them good men and women with young families, are desperate for work in an institution that has halved its size in ten years. Am I a traitor to those who kept me in work, my colleagues my profession and my class?

Brigadier General José Francisco Gallardo Rodriguez commanded the Equestrian Center of The Mexican Army. In 1989 he was accused of stealing four thousand US dollars worth of government horse feed. He was "cleared...of any wrongdoing"[2]. Then in 1993 these charges were "resurrected" and Gallardo additionally accused of destroying incriminating accounts. Subsequent to two courts martial, this officer was dishonorably deranked and sentenced to more than fifteen years in jail. I have just found another aging Reuters cable[3] that sets the scene by stating:-

MEXICO CITY, March 31 [1998] (Reuters) - Disappearances and extrajudicial executions in Mexico are on the rise, arbitrary detentions are frequent and torture is common, human rights organisations alleged on Monday.

Now it would appear that Gallardo's real offence was his public complaint about the torture and abuse of serving Mexican soldiers by their own comrades and his advocacy of a "human rights ombudsman" for enlisted men. Readers who find this incredible may recollect the current state of ferment in Mexico and some of the circumstances attending the state of war in the Chiapas region. Neither should the allegations of peculation give my readers too much pause for thought for as a former trades union official I well understand the machinations of corrupt minds and their stratagems against honest men.

Read yesterday's letter from Señora Leticia Gallardo:-

Tlalpan

August 11 1999

¡Hello James!
Today is a total eclipse of the sun,¡Congratulation!¡you may see it!

In other things James, I big your pardon because until this time I'm answering your beautiful post-card (December 97), thank you for the support to foster us to go on with the struggle of human rights defense. My husband, General Gallardo, prisoner of conscience, still keeps his spirit up, thanks to you.

General Gallardo has been transferred to a civil prison. Although it is still an imprisonment, we think it is to be looked upon as a good sign, but, we are worried because in this places, there are many delinquents and attempt revolt or other things.

This way, we think that now is a good time to write anew to mexican President, I send you his dress.

With my warm regards, and I hope you have a nice summer.

Yours Faithfully,
Leticia Enriquez de Gallardo

I am ashamed to admit that the Señora's English is far superior to my Spanish, so I replied in these terms:-

Bloxwich

September 1999
Dear Señora Gallardo

Thank you for your kind letter of August 11 1999. Thank you also for writing in English. I am sorry that my knowledge of Spanish is not good enough to reply in your language. You were right, I did see the eclipse of the Sun that day and it was a most unusual and moving experience though here in Central England the occlusion was only 94%.

Be assured that the courage and goodness of your Husband remains a celebration for, and an inspiration to, men and women of goodwill worldwide. He is an example who transcends distinctions of faith race nation or class and will ever be in thought and prayer until he is restored to his rightful place of honor in the Service of God and of his country. Your Husband has made great sacrifices to follow Him who first sought to be merciful and not to sacrifice and whatever life may bring to Brigadier General Gallardo his Faith shall not remain unrequited, nor shall his sufferings not bear fruit.

I have today written to Señor Ernesto Ponce de León to commend the restoration of your Husband to his high position of honor in your country for I believe that Brigadier General Gallardo has The Will of Christ and the welfare of His people at heart. I enclose a copy of my letter to your President.

I will continue to pray for the Serenity of your Husband and yourself and the Happiness of Mexico.

Va con Dios,
James R Warren

Readers may be interested to know that the Mexican Constitution specifically proscribes the participation of foreigners in internal affairs, and it is probably on that basis that forty (Vatican-accredited) priests have been deported from their parishes in the Chiapas. I did not know this when I chose to address Señor Zedillo in these terms:-

Bloxwich

8

September 1999
To The Most Excellent
El Presidente de la Republica de la (sic) Estados Unidos de Mexico
Señor Ernesto Zedillo Ponce de León

Your Excellency
   It is my distinct privilege to request Your Excellency to review the predicament of Brigadier General José Francisco Gallardo Rodriguez, a soldier of Mexico in peril.
   A foreigner ignorant of the successes and problems of the Mexican people is understandably embarrassed to canvass what may be construed an insolent regard for your affairs. I am not a member of any «pressure group» or political organisation. I am socially far inferior to your servant General Gallardo and probably have views very different from his. As a Quaker pacifist I abhor his chosen vocation, and, as a Englishman, I respect and salute Your Excellency's determination to resist interference by serving officers and your obvious rigor in upholding the Constitution of Mexico.
   I am an ordinary man who is begging a man of honor to show clemency to a compassionate and honest person who is in his power.
   Please release Brigadier General Gallardo to an honorable restoration of his rights and duties as a servant of your People because he is a good man who has tried to fulfill The Will of Christ as he understands it. ¿Can more be asked of us fallible men?
   Forgive my failure to write this letter in Spanish: My command of your language is so poor it would not do justice to an educated reader.
   May the Blessings of Our Divine Savior be upon Gallardo, Your Excellency and all of the People of Mexico, and Guide you always.

                    Va con Dios,
                    James R Warren

In the following month the Mexican Government replied:-

Palacio Nacional, 11 de Octubre de 1999.

F: 328988-58

SR. JAMES R. WARREN
31 VICTORIA AVENUE, BLOXWICH WALSALL, WS3 3HS, INGLATERRA

ESTIMADO SR. WARREN

A nombre del Sr. Presidente de la República , Ernesto Zedillo Ponce de León, me permito acusar recibo de su escrito en el que:
EXPRESA SU CONSTERNACION POR LA DETENCION DEL GENERAL BRIGADIER JOSE FRANCISCO GALLARDO RODRIGUEZ, ASIMISMO, DESEA SE ADOPTEN MEDIDAS PARA GARANTIZAR SU SEGURIDAD Y LA DE SU FAMILIA
Sobre el particular, sirva este conducto para informarle que el Sr. Presidente quedó enterado del contenido de su comunicación.

ATENTAMENTE
LA COORDINADORA DE ATENCION CIUDADANA

LIC. LEONOR ORTIZ MONASTERIO

I have translated this below, and whilst my rendition contains crudities due to my poor Spanish, it may capture the spirit of the reply:-

The National Palace, 11 October 1999

F: 328988-58

Mr James R Warren
31 Victoria Avenue, Bloxwich Walsall, WS3 3HS, England

My Dear Mr Warren

In the name of the President of the Republic, Ernesto Zedillo Ponce de León, permit me to acknowledge receipt of your document in which you:-

EXPRESS YOUR DISMAY AT THE DETENTION OF THE BRIGADIER GENERAL JOSE FRANCISCO GALLARDO RODRIGUEZ, ALSO, YOUR WISH FOR US TO TAKE MEASURES TO GUARANTEE HIS SECURITY AND THAT OF HIS FAMILY

Concerning the particular, I shall use the appropriate channel to certify that Mr President is well-informed of the contents of your communication.

Yours Sincerely
Ombudswoman

Leonor Ortiz Monesterio, LLB

Sources

1. Micah 6:8
2. "Mexico Tells OAS to Steer Clear of General Case"
   David Luhnow
   (Intercepted Reuters cable of 31 March 1998)
   http://burn.ucsd.edu/archives/chiapasI/1998.03/msg00628.html
3. "Rights Groups Say Torture, Abuse Endemic in Mexico"
   Anonymous
   (Intercepted Reuters cable of 31 March 1998)
   http://burn.ucsd.edu/archives/chiapas-I/1998.03/msg00627.html

Manumission

30 October 1999

The night of October 27 to 28 1999 in my house at Bloxwich.

As I lie in bed I dream that I am literally running publishers' errands in London during the First World War. The lifeless city rests beneath clouded KG5 skies. I run through a leafy park towards sixties office blocks clean and hyaline against the horizon. I run through daylit tunnels with tracks and smokeless silent steam trains. They are shallow oblong cut-and-fill tunnels unlike those vermicular Northern Line places. There are rusting cartridge cases on the ballast.

I awake.

I pray to Christ to understand His Love, His Scripture and the world we live in.

Involuntarily, but within less than a minute, I passively behold the English word "FREEDOM" written on every page of The Bible in varying sizes, cases and alignments like a gray computer watermark. It appears to expand and grow beyond the bounds of the turning flimsy pages whilst the indelible black text of Scripture remains.

I am delighted, I weep, and I do not understand.

We speak very glibly of liberty. Perhaps no single concept, not excluding God Himself, is today the object of so much cant and hypocrisy. But to the old men, as to our fathers, to allow freedom to slip from the grasp was to enter the world of Satan.

Pride and The Laws and pride in the law cannot shield us from unreason. We should remember this in an age when Science appears to carry all before her. The Romans were proud men who especially revered their own "justice". I have before me a beautifully-bound copy of "Adam's Roman Antiquities"[1] published at London in 1835. Listen to how The Romans elicited the facts before a judicial trial:-

1   QUÆSTIONES   The slaves of the defendant were demanded by the prosecutor to be examined by torture in several trials,...

...they were stretched on a machine called ECULEUS, or *Equuleus* having their legs and arms tied to it by ropes... their members were distended by means of screws (per cochleas), sometimes till they were dislocated (

ut ossium compago resolvereter)... To increase the pain, plates of red-hot iron (laninæ caudentes), pincers, burning pitch, &c. were applied to them...

    2 TESTES   Free citizens gave their testimony on oath (jurati).

  I hasten to reassure nervous readers that should a chattel be killed or incapacitated by questioning, the plaintiff was obliged to compensate the relevant owner. Nevertheless, in spite of this equitable provision, corrupt persons would frequently attempt to frustrate forensic process by pre-emptive manumission. The State had to step in. Augustus compulsorily-purchased intended victims, either personally or on behalf of the public.

  When we bear in mind that none of The Bible was penned after the Third Century AD and that slavery persisted well into the Christian Era we can sense the peculiar fascination which the idea of freedom exerted upon Ancient minds. Lest we remain in doubt about this matter, or think that the love of liberty was a late affectation, we may review the terms of The Second Book of Kings which may discuss events around 530 BC:-

  And he [Nebuchadnezzar king of Babylon] carried away all Jerusalem, and all the princes, and all the mighty men of valour, even ten thousand captives, and all the craftsmen and smiths: none remained, save the poorest sort of people of the land. And he carried away Jehoiachin to Babylon, and the king's mother, and the king's wives, and his officers, and the mighty of the land, those carried he into captivity from Jerusalem to Babylon.[a]

  As I read this passage I sensed a second time something peculiar, something foreign and demotic about the spirit of narration. This feeling had first struck me when I applied a computer search for the word "freedom" in the KJV text.

  Surprisingly, the machine found only two mentions. This is the first:-

  And whosoever lieth carnally with a woman, that is a bondmaid, betrothed to an husband, and not at all redeemed, nor freedom given her; she shall be scourged; they shall not be put to death, because she was not free.[b]

  This Law may date from Archaic times but is alien to postcedent Classical thought, not least because the betrothal of the bond was a legal contradiction to the Roman.

The plebeian interest of the treatment of freedom persists through a millennial jump to the other verse that cites freedom, part of Paul's celebrated conversation with the Roman soldier:-

And as they bound him with thongs, Paul said unto the centurion that stood by, Is it lawful for you to scourge a man that is a Roman, and uncondemned? When the centurion heard that, he went and told the chief captain, saying, Take heed what thou doest: for this man is a Roman. Then the chief captain came, and said unto him, Tell me, art thou a Roman? He said, Yea. And the chief captain answered, With a great sum obtained I this freedom. And Paul said, But I was free born. Then straightway they departed from him which should have examined him: and the chief captain also was afraid, after he knew that he was a Roman, and because he had bound him.[c]

How different is this Semitic emphasis to our aristocratic Greco-Roman tradition, to the strangely adolescent elitism of *The Republic*[2], or the callous disdain of Aristotle.

If we return to that Kings passage about the abduction of the Jews we can plainly see that the genius which penned that history was someone or something for whom the first would be last, and the last first. It may be no accident that the "craftsmen and smiths" have central place in the relation, preceding the king and the king's women. It may be no accident that true liberty emerged among a tribe whose manhood all learned a trade as a sacred duty and officiated without earthly recompense. It may be no accident that modern freedom flickered to life among artisans and tradesmen, glowed a little in the winds of commerce and venture, and died again in mass dependency.

What is the greatest freedom? How free is Herod as he enjoys his servile luxuries and bankrupt splendors and keeps his hireling kingship with ruthless cruelty? What is the secret desideratum of the beleaguered Idumean as he surveys his stolen glory and grasps fast his slipping crown? What enemy is it that afflicts all, even unto Nebuchadnezzar or Octavian?

Let us continue our exploration of liberty with the Author of The Second Book of Kings:-

And the King of Babylon made Mattaniah his father's brother king in his stead, and changed his name to Zedekiah.[d]

To a traditional man, for whom his name had totemistic portent, this would be no mere formality. It would confirm his utter destruction as an individual, whether or not aggravated by the intentional mockeries with which we used to name imported negroes. I am not a hebraist but it might be that Mattaniah means "gift of Yah" whilst Zedekiah may mean "Yah is might": Perhaps the name change bears an insult obscure to the modern reader. Perhaps it is merely a crude sneer. As Quakers we understand such things.

Kings continues a baleful narration of Zedekiah's offence of Yah (perhaps an apostasy) and of the nemesis exacted. Zedekiah rebels and is besieged for eleven years. The privations of siege in any age ensue. Then at last:-

So they took the king [Zedekiah], and brought him up to the king of Babylon to Riblah; and they gave judgment upon him. And they slew the sons of Zedekiah before his eyes, and put out the eyes of Zedekiah, and bound him with fetters of brass, and carried him to Babylon.[e]

An interesting sidelight upon these wars is thrown by Psalm 137, perhaps the most famous song ever sung, or at least the most sung religious song:-

> By the rivers of Babylon
> There we sat down, yea, we wept,
> When we remembered Zion.
> We hanged our harps
> Upon the willows in the midst thereof.
> For there they that carried us away captive
>   required of us a song;
> And they that wasted us required of us mirth, saying,
> Sing us one of the songs of Zion.
> How shall we sing the LORD'S song in a strange land?
> If I forget thee, O Jerusalem,
> Let my right hand forget her cunning.
> If I do not remember thee,
> Let my tongue cleave to the roof of my mouth;
> if I prefer not Jerusalem Above my chief joy.
> Remember O LORD, the children of Edom
> In the day of Jerusalem;
> Who said, Rase it, rase it,
> Even to the foundation thereof.
> O daughter of Babylon, who art to be destroyed;
> Happy shall he be, that rewardeth thee
> As thou hast served us.
> Happy shall he be, that taketh and dasheth thy little ones
> Against the stones.

We were told by the Ancients that Satan has very strong views about The Will of Man. We hardly need any to tell us that the wages of rape is hate and that the consummation of hate is death.

Verdi and Boito brought their own manifestos to this ancient scenario and their contemporary American negroes would have savored every political and religious nuance of the psalm. Twentieth-century schmaltzmongers have of course bowdlerised the text of all disquieting images.

But this old poem yearns with the nostalgia of the disinherited and has all the wistful fairness of the fallen angel. It does not say that Jews can serve God in their new home. For its limpid beauty is unlovely. It is the parable of desolation.

Yet men and women can turn the corner. For Psalm 139 rises with lark-like optimism to sing:-

> if I make my bed in hell, behold, thou art there.
> If I take the wings of the morning,
> and dwell in the uttermost parts of the sea;
> Even there shall thy hand lead me,
> And thy right hand shall hold me.

Given the democratic nature of the Jewish patrimony, their small numbers and their strategic position in a nodal but desert land it is not surprising that they were the constant prey of princely adventurers and their mounted hordes; the Egyptians, the Assyrians, the Babylonians, the Seleucids, the Romans; to name but the more splendid.

Whether or not they enjoyed Divine Tutelage, it is little wonder that they valued fraternity, continence and freedom. Yet now and then The Light of God himself glimmers through the glodes of their storm-swept writings and the smoke of their burning habitations to prefigure the Salvation of the Meek.

For flee as they might, even to the uttermost parts of the sea, they could not escape the hurricane which would transfigure a world:-

> I cried by reason of mine affliction unto the LORD, and he heard me; out of the belly of hell cried I, and thou heardest my voice. For thou hadst cast me into the deep, in the midst of the seas; and the floods compassed me about: all thy billows and thy waves passed over me. Then I said, I am cast out of thy sight; yet I will look again toward thy holy temple. The waters compassed me about, even to the soul: the depth closed me round about, the weeds were wrapped about my head. I went down to the bottoms of the mountains; the earth with her bars was about me for ever: yet hast thou brought up my life from corruption, O LORD my

God. When my soul fainted within me I remembered the LORD: and my prayer came in unto thee, into thine holy temple. They that observe lying vanities forsake their own mercy. But I will sacrifice unto thee with the voice of thanksgiving; I will pay that that I have vowed. Salvation is of the LORD.[f]

Corruption. That is an interesting word. When decay and depravity are everywhere. When the councils of Caesar are full of wide-boys and witlings. When all has a price but nought has value and the honest oppressed and the sycophantic preferred: Where then is the Last Refuge of the reasonable man?
Paul thought he had the answer:

Being then made free from sin, ye become the servants of righteousness. I speak after the manner of men because of the infirmity of your flesh: for as ye have yielded your members servants to uncleanness and to iniquity unto iniquity; even so now yield your members servants to righteousness unto holiness. For when ye were the servants of sin, ye were free from righteousness. What fruit had ye then in those things whereof ye are now ashamed? for the end of these things is death. But now being made free from sin, and become servants to God, ye have your fruit unto holiness, and the end everlasting life. For the wages of sin is death; but the gift of God is eternal life through Jesus Christ our Lord.[g]

When the Greco-Roman world was yielding to Stoic despair a sunrise was dawning from the East, an optimism that for those with courage to abandon politics, prosperity, pragmatism and the toils of the flesh a new dispensation of perpetual liberty would supersede.
Augustine was abroad: "Love God and do as you like". For what is more firmly bound than a slave to the works of the world?

But Jerusalem which is above us is free, which is the mother of us all.[h]

So what is the source of bondage? It is fear. For fear is the inspiration of cowardice, the father of all evils. Fear of poverty, fear of contempt, fear of bondage, fear of fear itself. To be freed of fear is to be freed:-

Then said Jesus to those Jews which believed on him, If ye continue in my word, then are ye my disciples indeed; And ye shall know the truth, and the truth shall make you free. They answered him, We be Abraham's seed, and were never in bondage to any man: how sayest thou, Ye shall be made free? Jesus answered them, Verily, verily, I say unto you, Whosoever committeth sin is the servant of sin. And the servant abideth not in the house for ever: but the Son abideth ever. If the Son therefore shall make you free, ye shall be free indeed.[i]

Acknowledgement

I am indebted to David A Bayliss for the provision of the computer KJV search tool SamFindex V1.08.1 (Copyright: David A Bayliss, 1988-91), which was used to identify the readings cited here.

References

1. "Roman Antiquities; Or,
   An Account of the Manners and Customs of the Romans"
   Alexander Adam, LLD
   Rector of The High School Edinburgh
   Twelfth Edition
   1835
   (page 226)

2. "The Republic"
   Plato
   Translated by Desmond Lee
   Second (Revised) Edition   1974
   Penguin Books Limited of Harmondsworth
   ISBN 0-14-044.048-8

Readings

a   2 Kings 24:14-15
b   Leviticus 19:20
c   Acts 22:25-29
d   2 Kings 24:17
e   2 Kings 25:7
f   Jonah 2:2-9
g   Romans 6:18-23
h   Galatians 4:26
i   John 8:31-37

Perdition's Illusion

11 March 2000

Many Sundays ago, when I was an undergraduate, I collapsed in post-prandial torpor into a leather chair in my hall. I listlessly leafed the thick and heavy Sabbath papers, for I was a poor student and idle. One of the papers ran a strip cartoon. (Why it was so styled I never discovered, for its protagonists were always naked). Adam and Eve completed six days labor with naïf predictability but one day was an exception. Eve was standing below her tree from which a single apple depended. A sleek and mottled snake appeared from aloft and said to our primogenitrix "Eat this lovely apple". Eve coyly replied "No, God doesn't want me to", whereupon the Wily One objected "God doesn't really exist: He is merely a projection of your subconscious". Her youthful face transformed with rage, The Mother of Men turned to an abashed serpent and screamed "You are a wicked, wicked demon to tempt a pious maiden - and what is far, far worse, you are an intellectual!".

I suppose Søren Kierkegaard was an intellectual's intellectual, but if he was a wicked wicked demon then he was a lonely and disconsolate one. Søren broke an engagement with his only love for which he never forgave himself and though the young lady promptly repaired to the Danish Virgin Islands with a rich suitor her memory would haunt the theologian's writings all his remaining days. And yet Kierkegaard was no wan and neurasthenic Chatterton. It is hard to imagine that one with his humor and optimism would find no mate yet The Father of Existentialism spent the rest of his years spurned or satirised in genteel penury.

Learning in Berlin at the feet of Hegel, Kierkegaard became the sworn enemy of the systematic rationalism that that rectilinear Prussian philosopher apotheosised, and turned head on to face down alone the whole enormous prospectus of Teutonic world-historical determinism which was to underpin the monstrous ideologies of our unlamented Twentieth-Century.

The Kant-Hegel system was itself a debasement of the Carteso-Newtonian synthesis of the Seventeenth-Century, and like all debasements tendentiously sought to import scientific or religious authority into a foreign dialectic.

Lest you think that this is a dour Dane of whom I write, remote and antique in some provincial aridity, let me show you some graphic work of filmic felicity in which Kierkegaard paints a busy picture of the Copenhagen street and the Life beyond it:-

> "When Johannes sometimes asked for permission to go out, he was most often refused; but occasionally, as if to make up for this refusal, the father proposed a walk together up and down the room. This seemed at first a poor substitute; and yet, like his father's coarse gray coat, it concealed under its plain exterior something very different from that which appeared on the surface. The proposal accepted, it was for Johannes himself to decide where to go. They passed out the gate and visited a neighboring palace; or went to the seashore, or wondered about the streets, all at the boy's pleasure. For the father's imagination was powerful enough to create a realizing sense of anything and everything the boy desired. While they walked up and down, the father described the sights along the way; they greeted the passers-by; the vehicles rumbled and drowned the father's voice; the dainties displayed by the fruitwoman on the corner seemed more alluring than ever. When they were on ground familiar to Johannes everything was given a description so vivid and minute that not the smallest detail was overlooked."[1]

With words alone a genius has more than adumbrated the crowded animation of "Heaven's Gate" or the artful balletics of a Ken Russell. And yet these lone words shadow forth a much more profound Reality of a boy or man in the Realm of a Loving Father.

Some readers will be more than aware of a few of the infinite hidden pitfalls which lurk in wait for the student of existence, for even at an elementary mathematical level the way is fraught with error. Descartes told us that he had proven the existence of God, and yet considered his own being tenuous enough to depend upon *cogito ergo sum*.

Søren's dictum was more like "I feel therefore I am" though of course this too falls short of guaranteeing the actuality of men who move as shadows across the hollow scrim of a scene, glimpsing the Reality of some superior Dimension whose Creatures find equal difficulty in Visiting the chimerical world we inhabit. For a few minutes which seem like years men and women swagger a while and shamble from the stage to resume their essential substance as smoke and steam or occasionally perhaps the ptomaic liquors and soils which also contribute to sustain little animals and tiny plants in the hidden gardens of the sepulchre. Yet Kierkegaard is speaking to us today, as clearly as he could ever manage, using as he did a tongue evolved for sailors and shepherds, discussing as he did the uttermost bournes of human comprehension.

For Kierkegaard, decision was the quintessential psychospiritual discriminator of humanity[a], a God-given corollary of the Free Will promised by a Judge who Loves. But the natural concomitant of choice is error. Satan introduced Adam and Eve to Error, and Error makes Justice, Truth and even Freedom itself problematic to mortal men. The lurking presence of Error forever makes Knowledge impossible, necessitating Kierkegaard's much-canvassed "Leap of Faith".

And if men can hope and love and pray who are we to surmise that Søren's only vestige is the revenant memory of mortal minds?

For what is life? And what is life like? I do not know what Life is but Life is like yesterday at Minninglow where as I peered over the flank of the grassy kist-crowned hill I saw a circle of six unmapped Neolithic standing stones I had not realised were there. Gray in the vernal sun lay they, Dinantian limestone sarsens honed round by the howling hail of ages. Gray as the drystone dykes and ice-plucked slabs and quarry walls about me. Always curious about antique things I strode against the freezing wind to see them, and they raised their heads and skittered in alarm.

The final letter from my Late Mother stated:-

"For goodness sake do not forget the certainty of death. I've had a good life and have a pride in a worthy son; so go on with your life and I wish you better health and loads of good luck. Keep happy and keep walking!"

The valediction of she who gave me life was this, for we can barely see over the col and that we discern may be a mirage. The massage of Man is the certitude of Death.

But if the very stones can rise and scatter who are we to question The Resurrection of the Flesh?

Kierkegaard had a reciprocal approach to Descartes:-

"A sense of intellectual bankruptcy impelled the reputed father of modern philosophy to seek a radical reconstruction of the basic concepts of science...

In Kierkegaard we have a thinker who completely reverses the Cartesian distribution of emphasis: he reflects where Descartes accepts, and accepts where Descartes reflects. He took his point of departure in something deeper than an abstract intellectual doubt, namely, in a concrete personal despair. In this despair, which was ironically witty and articulate, he questioned the meaning and truth of human life in its whole range of substantial values. The struggle to find solid ground under his feet was undertaken with a concentration of all his faculties, intellectual and passional; and, in gradually achieving this task for himself, he brought into being a revision of the basic categories of human existence."[3]

But it is this concrete personal despair which is the harbinger of all true Faith, for conviction can only appear through the travail of The Cross, and not even Descartes could think Christ into existence.

So far ahead of his time was Kierkegaard that he anticipated some of the twentieth-century's reservations about the attainability of knowledge, especially in the rôle of the observer and his concomitant postulate, (one may almost call it an essential license), of objectivity.

In 1846, Kierkegaard's prolific outpourings of pamphlets and apologia culminated in his *Concluding Unscientific Postscript to* **Philosophical Fragments**, a 630-page afterthought in sequel to a much shorter book. Part Two Section II Chapter I opens with:-

"Objectively, one continually speaks only about the case in point; subjectively, one speaks about the subject and subjectivity - and see, the subjectivity itself is the case in point. It must continually be insisted upon that the subjective issue is not something about the case in point but is the subjectivity itself. In other words, since the issue is the decision and all decision, as shown previously, is rooted in subjectivity, it is important that objectively there be no trace whatever of any case in point, because at that very moment the subjective individual wants to evade some of the pain and crisis of decision, that is, wants to make the issue somewhat objective. If the introductory intellectual discipline is waiting for one more book before the matter is submitted to judgment, if the system lacks one more paragraph, if the speaker holds one more argument in reserve - then the decision is postponed. Thus there is not a question of the truth of Christianity here in the sense that if this was decided the subjective individual would then be ready and willing to accept it. No, the question is about the subject's acceptance of it. And here it must be regarded as perdition's illusion (which has remained ignorant of the fact that the decision is rooted in subjectivity) or as an equivocation of illusiveness (which shoves off the decision by objective treatment in which there is no decision in all eternity) to assume that this transition from something objective to a subjective acceptance follows directly of its own accord, since precisely this is the decisive point and an objective acceptance (*sit venia verbo* [pardon the expression]) is paganism or thoughtlessness."[2]

Science, pretender to the prophet's ancient staff of rectitude, sought at first to arrogate the observer's immutant throne at the fixed center of evolutions from which all existence in exactitudes could determinately be charted, self-contingent and mutually-explanatory without reference to Expositor or auditor. The Age of Elegance dreamt Newton's Sleep for a hundred years but by Kierkegaard's time the first cracks in the grand conspectus were starting to appear. Alternative geometries, based upon selective relaxations of the Euclidean axioms, had already been offered to a bemused public, and the Laplacian Order was doomed.

Henceforth, The Age of Progress would celebrate a brief marriage with The Equivocation of Illusiveness, admitting that no final certitude was accessible, but that ever convergent approximations of truth would build ever ascending spires of knowledge on foundations of:- foundations of what? Basalt or Sand?

Then one brilliantly starlit freezing night, an unsinkable ship sailed majestically upon its first voyage into Mid-Atlantic and gracefully sank. The Age of Uncertainty was born.

During the last two hundred years we have played-out the great world-historical drama which Kant, Hegel and their British imitators published. The satanic mills of socio-cultural determinism have ground forth the chaff of fascism, Marxism and all manner of neo-Darwinian and pseudo-Darwinian clap-trap which is, after killing more than seventy million, thankfully dying with the old century but lingers in the more unreconstructed back-waters of Anglo-American applied science and agribusiness.

Kierkegaard must have been at least two hundred years ahead of his time in, like Blake, questioning the rationalist world-view and its vision for humanity. But, unlike Blake, the Dane could sustain a complex critique with humor and without diatribe though admittedly also without elegance or compassion.

I say "at least two hundred" because we still have not really begun to work out the implications of the Existential world-view. For sure, Sartre, Camus and other French modernists have explored the implications of "Atheistic Existentialism" but having not read these I am unable to assess their work. There is the more than latent danger, felt in full force in the decadent years of Prussian rationalism, that, as Dr Feelgood strangles Dr Strangelove, vulgarisation of the Existential prospectus is already engendering a "me-first" secular hedonism. If we are to fill the void left by the death of the isms whilst averting the paradigm of mindless materialism and cynical opportunism we must satisfy again Man's need for Faith as well as Logic.

Note

a   We now know that there is nothing distinctively human about this cybernetic operation, but readers may recollect that as Kierkegaard penned his grand summary, George Boole was a struggling teacher three years away from promotion to the famine-struck obscurity of Cork; Babbage had given up trying to interest The Admiralty in difference engines; and Ada Lovelace had resumed the aristocratic anonymity of her married life.
Later work confirmed the age-old wisdom that non-human animals could make decisions, and did so habitually.

References

1   *De omnibus dubitandum est*
   Unpublished manuscript by Søren Kierkegaard
   1842-43
   in
   "The 'Literature' - A Resume"   (p 71)
   "Something about Kierkegaard"
   David F Svenson
   Augsburg Publishing House of Minneapolis   1941
   (ROSE reprint of Mercer University Press,
     1983)
   ISBN 0-86554-084-5

2   "Concluding Unscientific Postscript to
   Philosophical Fragments"
   "[A Mimical-Pathetical-Dialectical Compilation
     An Existential Contribution]"
   Søren Kierkegaard
   (pseudonymously Johannes Climacus)
   Copenhagen, February 1846
   Edited and Translated by HV and EH Hong
   Princeton University Press, New Jersey   1992
   ISBN 0-691-07395-3
   pp 129-130   VII104-VII105

3   IV. The Existential Dialectic of Søren Kierkegaard
   (p 111)
   in
   "Something about Kierkegaard"
   David F Svenson
   Augsburg Publishing House of Minneapolis   1941
   (ROSE reprint of Mercer University Press,
     1983)
   ISBN 0-86554-084-5

The Fishes of Rimini

2 December 2000

When wise men wish to understand the grandest evolutions of the cosmos, or descry more closely the Will of God, they always consult the animals.

Our Holy Savior was neither the first nor the last to heed their silent counsel when He said (Matthew 6:26):-

"Behold the fowls of the air: for they sow not, neither do they reap nor gather into barns; yet your heavenly Father feedeth them".

Though proud with others Aristotle did not disdain the sea-urchin. White observed the habits of the creatures in the environs of his living, whilst Wallace and Darwin risked life itself to learn of foreign finches or jungle troupes. Miller went to greater lengths and learned the lore of "tiny boatmen" for ever ageless in his Old Red Sandstone.

Ages of Reason and of Progress would question the sanity of learned men who addressed ruder creatures in Romance tongues, but such proprieties did not trouble St Anthony of Padua:-

CHRIST the blessed, being pleased to show forth the great holiness of His most faithful servant, St. Anthony, and with what devotion his preaching and his holy doctrine were to be heard, one time, among others, rebuked the folly of infidel heretics by means of creatures without reason, to wit, the fishes;

For some days the Franciscan had been locked in fruitless confutations with the dissident townsfolk of Rimini, and you can see the anger and fatigue on Anthony's frustrated face as a million fascinated little children must have envisaged it as they were lulled to sleep by pious parents down nine succeeding centuries.

Unforgettably, the saint made a leap from the bounds of his own logical reference frame of a character that would win temporal immortality for a thousand later sages:-

Wherefore St. Anthony, by divine inspiration, went one day to the bank of the river, hard by the seashore, and standing there on the bank of the river, between it and the sea, began to speak to the fishes after the manner of a preacher sent by God, "Hear the word of God, ye fishes of the sea and of the river, since the miscreant heretics scorn to hear it". And when he had thus spoken, anon there came towards the bank such a multitude of fishes, great and small, and middling, that never before in those seas, nor in that river, had so great a multitude been seen; and all held their heads out of the water in great peace and gentleness and in perfect order, and remained intent on the lips of St. Anthony: for in front of him and nearest to the bank were the lesser fishes; and beyond them were those of middling size; and then behind, where the water was deepest, were the greater fishes.

One needs to doubt no particular of this sensational narrative to admire the skill of the master iconographer who contrasts the chaos of human discord with the divine order and intention of these serious listeners "without reason". Or of the felicity of circumstance of those able to swim from the brine of becoming to the sweet waters of salvation.

This little flower further unfolds as Anthony, not forgetting the dignity, the liberty, and the independence of his audience chooses to preach a homily very much *ad piscem*:-

The fishes being then mustered in such order and array, St. Anthony began to preach to them solemnly, and spake thus, "Ye fishes, my brothers, much are ye held, according to your power, to thank God our Creator, who hath given you so noble an element for your habitation; for at your pleasure have ye waters, sweet and salt, and He hath given you many places of refuge to shelter you from the tempests; He hath likewise given you a pure and clear element, and food whereby ye can live. God, your Creator, bountiful and kind, when He created you, commanded you to increase and multiply, and gave you His blessing; then, in the universal deluge and when all other animals were perishing, you alone did God preserve from harm. Moreover, He hath given you fins that ye may fare whithersoever it may please you."

My Wife Jana has a fishpond in which she keeps goldfish and other ornamental carp. These fish have but a little compass but obey all these admonitions according to their power, just as it is futile to urge any of us to transgress the limits of our element, though we may change its savor. Jana kindly provided lily leaves as little parasols and strange to relate the fishes shelter from the deluge beneath these seemingly redundant roofs. When my Wife or I stand at the corner of the pond the fishes silently and suddenly foregather, their plump faces serenely looking up at us with guileless expectation, for they reason that a dole of food may well be imminent. And when a twelfth-century monk congratulates fish for surviving *the* Deluge it is salutary to remember the work that Miller pioneered, proving to a secular age that fish are the only chordates to arrive alive from the Devonian, surviving several extinctions in which other orders have vanished wholesale[a].

Sounding more deeply the privy mysteries of these Favored creatures, Anthony regales more intimately his rapt audience:-

"To you it was granted, by commandment of God, to preserve Jonah the prophet, and after the third day to cast him forth on dry land, safe and whole. Ye did offer the tribute money to Christ our Lord, to Him, poor little one, that had not wherewithal to pay. Ye, by a rare mystery, were the food of the eternal King, Christ Jesus, before the resurrection and after. For all those things much are ye held to praise and bless God, that hath given you blessings so manifold and so great; yea, more even than to any other of His creatures".

Note that there is not a trace of condescension in Anthony's address. Christ Jesus is *our*, human, Lord Whom the fishes help. The fish are perfectly free to reverence their own Christ if that is meet. The fish are doing *us* all the favors. And by a yet more difficult turn the fish Sustain our Savior both before and after his biological death.

Anthony shares with Jesus Christ the perspective that animals are autonomous Children of God, whom they serve and praise directly. Some of the classical naturalists of The Enlightenment sailed close to this vision, so utterly at variance with the soulless instrumentalism embraced by Genesis and the modern man.

It was of course at this juncture that a thousand alert boys and girls queried the apparent asymmetry of doctrine, earning the inevitable but richly unmerited clip round the ear. Clearly, equity requires that were the fish to discover a Christ of their own, and were He to happen to be a large predator, say a shark, then it would be meet for him to partake of men, both in His earthly life and after His Resurrection.

Once again, a superficially ludicrous doctrinal confection conceals some very unfunny implications.

The patriarchs and prophets of the Old Testament labored through centuries to remove the horror of human sacrifice, baleful in its results for both the psychic and ecological conditions of man. How many Innocents have been killed, both in our Teutonic sphere and in alien cultures, to propitiate Moloch, serpent-gods, fish-gods and legions of bestial idols? And yet Anthony does not congratulate the fishes for their sacrifice and their suffering but for their sustentative collaboration as it were as equals in a most sublime and mysterious project. For Our Savior came to offer *Himself* in the final and culminating Sacrifice of which the Eucharist is the appointed remembrance.

In the Summer of 1998 Jana and I crossed the Northern border back into England. Like many of the marcher provinces of Europe, Cumberland displays a wistful desolation and strangely archaic installations as if peoples would expend no effort upon debatable ground. We left the motorway and drove East through avenues of great oaks winding through well-built hamlets of finely-pointed gritstone ashlar. The golden sun shone down from a cloudless sky as we passed over a wooden-gated level crossing beside which a chocolate-and-cream signal box with engrailed barge-boards guarded semaphore signals, a scene altogether reminiscent of the residual railroad about Aswan. But the heat of Cumberland was less intense and more intolerable than that of Nubia as we neared the fertile lowland lake of Talkin Tarn and parked.

My Wife and I walked through its fringing groves of dusty Scots pine to see the black and beverage-hot expanse of shallow water ripple far away to the South between undulating pastures.

It was a holiday and creatures without reason, to wit, men and boys, dangled hooks from the perimeter path. Sleek European perch hovered in the bank-side shallows gazing at the mercurial shimmer of the interface between our world and theirs like men seeking to peer outwith a black hole. Every now and then muffled rumbles and attenuated vociferations would herald a sudden puncture of the surface as idle cruelty mocked the fishs' desire for life. One man beside the path had a large haul of these fat and lustrous predators with their beautiful blazons of green and gold body bars and delicate red fins. Jana asked him how he was going to cook them. (The European perch is a most sumptuous dish for gentlemen, I am told. I have not been able to corroborate this for the obvious reason!). With embarrassed guilt the champion "fisherman" explained that he was fishing for pleasure and that all the fish would be returned to the lake dead or alive. Jana was indignant and admonished him for torturing the fish to null effect. He made no reply.

The perch has few fancy desires. He builds his nest, fertilises his beloved's eggs and guards his young, feeding only when he must. Though he lives through death, death and torment are never his *choice*. For Damnation and Redemption are both elections and living through imperatives never enlightened by Knowledge or made peccant by error all fish are Unfallen and none require a Savior upon their own behalf. No fish is therefore evil. Yet all fish have Reason, for this faculty is needed rightly to select the right actions upon which the biological survival of the individual (and through her the species) depends. Given the *choice* between life and death, pain and content, Man alone will, at leisure, chose pain and death.

The fishes of Rimini were highly delighted at Anthony's appreciative words for:-

At these and the like words and admonitions from St. Anthony, the fishes began to open their mouths and bow their heads, and by these and other tokens of reverence, according to their fashion and power, they gave praise to God...

...And the longer St. Anthony preached, the greater the multitude of fishes increased, and none departed from the place he had taken. And the people of the city began to run to behold this miracle,...

The townsfolk were amazed and the "heretics" withal obediently remained to hear Anthony's preaching. Then at length:-

This done, St. Anthony dismissed the fishes, with God's blessing, and all they departed with wondrous signs of gladness, and the people likewise.

Note

a   Certain worm-like forms such as Tunicata may even pre-date the five piscine orders, and Rhipidistian-derived amphibia crawled ashore at the close of the era.

Reference

"The Little Flowers of St Francis"
(published with "The Mirror of Perfection"
  by Leo of Assisi and "The Life of St Francis" by
  St Bonaventura: And with an introduction by the
  translator to English, Thomas Okey)
Everyman's Library
Dent and Dutton: London and New York: 1910

(From the *Fioretti*, Italian-language translations
  of the original Latin
  "Actus B. Francisci et sociorum ejus")

pp70-72
Chapter XL
"Of the Miracle that God wrought, when St. Anthony, being at Rimini, preached to the fishes in the sea"

Was Juniper a Woodentop?

8 December 2000

On a time as Friar Juniper was journeying to Rome, where the fame of his holiness was already noised abroad, many Romans, of their great devotion, went out to meet him; and Friar Juniper, beholding so many people coming, imagined how he might turn their devotion into sport and mockery. Now there were two children playing at see-saw, to wit, they had placed one log of wood across another, and each of them sat at his end of the log and see-sawed up and down. Away goes Friar Juniper and takes off one of these children from the log, and mounting thereon begins to play see-saw. Meanwhile the people came up and marvelled to see Friar Juniper see-sawing, yet, with great devotion, they greeted him and waited for him to end the game of see-saw, in order to accompany him honourably as far as the friary. And Friar Juniper heeded little their greetings, their reverence, and their waiting, but held very diligently to his see-sawing. And waiting thus a long space, certain of them began to weary thereof, and said, "What a blockhead"! Others, knowing his ways, waxed in greater devotion. Nevertheless all departed and left Friar Juniper on his see-saw. And when they were all gone, Friar Juniper was left wholly comforted, because he saw that certain of them had mocked at him. He then set forth and entered Rome, and with all meekness and humility came to the house of the friars minor.

Thus with childlike acceptance an unknown annalist continues the hagiography of his great, dead friends: They whom the Spanish would remember as San Bernardino, Santa Clara, San Francisco and San Antonio. With droll charm, his adze of atrament builds yet another window into the minds of men who would found a country called California, and yet spurn the fortunes along the river of their Queen of the Angels of the Small Portion.

As with the tale of Anthony and his fishes it is delightful to imagine the glee of little children as this simply hilarious and deeply disturbing story was read to them at bedtime.

Of course, the holy friar was not the first, and neither would he be the last, to enter Rome with all meekness and humility. How many torn and naked captives were dragged through the dust in triumph, or how many starved and goaded creatures *ad ludum*, we will not know this side of the grave. When challenged before the Appian Gate by an aging slave, Our Savior Himself replied that he entered to be re-crucified, and such has been the fate, physical or spiritual, of many who presented there.

And yet there is something engaging, homely and irrepressibly plebeian about these heirs of grandeur who would as indifferently mock or venerate a learned superior and as uncritically dismiss as accept his inexplicable message.

We are not told the sex of the child displaced, but he was of course a boy, and we wonder, in common with a million and one small girls, whether he ran blurting and snivelling to his mother at being so peremptorily frustrated; or whether he stood aside with manful gravitas, watching with knowing eyes the farce unfold, and judging the real as well as the ostensible follies around him.

But is it humility to seek how to turn devotion into sport and mockery or is it a vain delight in power masquerading as humility? For to abase himself is to act upon the Self with self-solicitude whilst true humbleness waits upon The Will of Christ and accepts whatever He confers whether that be empires or oubliettes. What of the faith and devotion of those who would have celebrated Juniper's entry into the City of Peter? Was Juniper justified in thinking their acclamation idolatrous, and scrupulous to be no Franciscan Naylor, to thus rudely defuse their zeal? And why, in that arena of all others, was to play see-saw so grave a degradation, so childish a sport so sullying?

Where is the humility and where the manly grace, native or Conferred, in removing a child from his delight to abase oneself or even to deliver an eternal homily?

"What a blockhead", we might well agree.

And yet the diverse acceptance and common desertion of the holy brother in his tiny passion postfigures a larger story and a greater remembrance, and if the antics of this weird friar minor have brought just one more child to the feet of his Savior then his childish guile gave wisest gain.

Reference

"The Little Flowers of St Francis"
(published with "The Mirror of Perfection"
  by Leo of Assisi and "The Life of St Francis" by
  St Bonaventura: And with an introduction by the
  translator to English, Thomas Okey)
Everyman's Library
Dent and Dutton: London and New York: 1910

(From the *Fioretti*, Italian-language translations
  of the original Latin
  "Actus B. Francisci et sociorum ejus")

p144
Section IX of The Life of Friar Juniper
"How Friar Juniper, to abase himself,
  played at see-saw."

The Road to Bedford Gaol

17 February 2001

Timelessly you park your car in the shortening shadow of Shevington's Saxon steeple. The pristine diamanté of the sparkling frost chills the silent limestone houses as tiny birds bob about their breakfasts in crannied litter.

The dissolving market cross passes you abeam as you amble down the rough hewn buttressed wall which retains the consecrated dead. The naked branches of a flanking copse blur shifting shapes in the warming Vernal sunlight on the slippery puddled slope.

In the laneside thickets throstles essay their aubade auguries and relent to audit our footfall.

I slide to stumble and you reach out to save me. I am glad you are here. Could I, like Winthrop, leap to storm-swept rocks to try conclusions with sharing savages in a wilderness, or like Penn find the courage to offer the open hand of equity to such as they? Or might I like Prynne mock the bigot's brand or keep with Fox dark oblivion shin-deep in excrement? No.

For whilst birds can love without question, men must trust despite appearances, or lie the aesthete skeptic mis-shriven and alone in the congress of the churchyard.

I am a flock animal. You are my companion.

The dark and viscid vortices of the distant silty river charm with defied lethality and nocturnal immersions a faithful vigil, freezing sanctuary alike to fallen men and floating fowl.

The matutinal mists afar discover a flock of waders slowly strutting with stilted deliberation through the steeping willowed meadow. All scale is lost in backlit haze as you define coots, or maybe water-hen, white-capped and black-pinioned in their guarding fen.

Yet already the younger game have gained the flood-plain's berm and pause on rising ground to scan bedappled; piebald apparitions like milling magpies, stately yet furtive.

John slouches up this slight acclivity from the misty Ouse ayonder. The bonneted women pass with murine discretion as he pauses at Bridget's sacred spring where the sweet, refractive waters have ever slaked the blind. His next bridewell will give him inner sight, and you and I a masterpiece.

All are soaked but do not shiver. John says "hedges have eyes" and the spies of Star Chamber peer unseen from every cleft and covert in the aging fabric of the landscape.

Seeker, you came to search for John, yet God's Grace is but the Precursor as I am a mere pursuivant. John's words garland the world, following the counsel of his beloved Hero. John is a tinker by trade and waits at the wayside for that Carpenter, for they build an innovation. We remain to plow the pregnant plains, wait on our Lord, and hope for laurels in heaven.

The many-striped blazon of a new republic takes life among us and we are content.

For Shevington is Everywhere and Nowhere, the Calvary of All Men, and we are yet to reach the Cross.

Arrested on King Street

29 October 2001

  I seldom open my mouth unless I put my foot in it. This is a decided debility when attending job interviews. Many an exciting and profitable university appointment have I forgone when nervousness has led to dumb inanities or hesitant confusions sometimes interpreted as arrogance.
  For rather than men, I prefer to speak to my strengths and those strengths devolve from the barrel of a propelling pencil.
  These twenty years I was employed as a lecturer at an obscure local college until a dwindling roll and a changing rôle combined to ensure my redundancy.
  Now again I require to convince the sceptical face-to-face. So I decided to seek training in the arts of the job interview to mitigate my weakness.
  Such training is rarer than you may think around Birmingham, but when I was threatened with termination twelve-months ago, I somehow found a firm called Impact Training Limited which seemed to offer such schooling.
  When this month dismissal became a reality I telephoned them to see if I could join a job interview class. The gentleman at the other end of the line spoke with an educated Wolverhampton accent and stated that such a class ran at a superannuated primary school in Blower's Green Road every Thursday from ten till one. After I had established that there would be no charge, I asked to enrol and he advised me simply to turn up. Meanwhile, he would tell the teacher to expect me.
  The morning of Thursday 18th October 2001 dawned dull. October is my favorite month, but she bears a leaden vintage in the streets and skies of the English Black Country. I wished my Wife good bye and caught a brace of buses through the somber housing wastes and over the low raddled hills of the former forge and foundry lands to Dudley.
  I was early and I paced the silence of the soaking streets past boarded shops, the ever-silent cinemas and the karate clubs, past the gauntly inaccessible sandstone church and the even more forbidding redbrick bunker of the Netto store.

At nine forty I entered the deserted modern foyer of the old school, dominated by a well-kept snooker table, and gingerly checked the complex of corridors and classrooms beyond. No-one was there.

In the foyer a notice board displayed over-cheerful colored cartoon faces working comic microcomputers with impossible delight. It said in text, in case there was lingering ambiguity, that Impact Training Limited was an initiative of The Afro-Caribbean and Friends Community aimed to address the needs of the local Blacks whose job market problems are particularly acute: One of the few tendentious and unsubstantiable assertions I have never found a need to doubt.

I read this with a heavy heart. I thought "this is not for me" and walked out.

Scripture is full of tales of great men in a distant past who turned their backs and ran, or rather tried to run and failed, and Our Savior was amongst those latter.

One of my favorites is the brief but perfect history of Jonah. You will recall that God commissioned this Israelite to preach His love to the sinful city of Nineveh, whereupon our hero took ship for far Tarshish. A violent storm overtook the frail vessel and to appease Divine Wrath Jonah consented to be jettisoned. He was instantly swallowed by an enormous marine creature of uncertain phylogeny. Jonah's prayer from "the belly of the whale" is one of the master works of sacred writing:-

> *Then Jonah prayed to the LORD his God out of the fish's belly,*
> *And said, I cried by reason of mine affliction unto the LORD,*
> > *and he heard me;*
> *out of the belly of hell cried I, and thou heardest my voice.*
> *For thou hadst cast me into the deep, in the midst of the seas;*
> > *and the floods compassed me about:*
> > *all thy billows and thy waves passed over me.*
> *Then I said, I am cast out of thy sight;*
> > *yet I will look again toward thy holy temple.*
> *The waters compassed me about, even to the soul:*
> > *the depth closed me round about,*
> > *the weeds were wrapped about my head.*
> *I went down to the bottoms of the mountains;*
> *The earth with her bars was about me for ever:*

> *yet hast thou brought up my life from corruption, O LORD my God.*
>
> *When my soul fainted within me I remembered the LORD:*
> *and my prayer came in unto thee, into thine holy temple.*
> *They that observe lying vanities forsake their own mercy.*
> *But I will sacrifice unto thee with the voice of thanksgiving;*
> *I will pay that that I have vowed.*
> *Salvation is of the LORD.*
> *And the LORD spake unto the fish,*
> *and it vomited out Jonah upon the dry land.*[a]

On regaining the light and lands of the Lord, Jonah wasted no more time in fulfilling his commission, and the happy people of Nineveh embraced the ways of God and were saved.

I walked back up Blower's Green Road and onto King Street. The day was as desolate as it had been, busy with machines but devoid of visible life.

But all around were tokens of The Cross. There were the vivid blue and yellow steel transoms and mullions of the shattered safety glass sides of the bus shelters; the rusting iron gallows of the old street lamps or perhaps long-unrigged tram catenaries; the intersecting aggers of the roads' carfaxes; even the anti-slip studs of the cast-iron manhole covers and stopcock hatches.

For suffering too is ubiquitous, as omnipresent as the Hope Jonah found inside his whale.

I am not normally a racist. At any rate, I respect the dark-skinned people of African descent. How can I forget the cheerful affability and uncomplaining industry of my many black students of former years, most of them gentle church-going people, seldom intellectual but always unpretentious?

How could I now succumb to my own prejudice and cowardice? If I fled now, surely I would fly from the much more urgent horrors of a job interview?

I knew that if I started to run now, I would run and run, and run for ever.

I turned back.

The kindly teacher and her softly-spoken students welcomed me. She commenced the lesson by giving me a cup of coffee. In thirty-three years of academic life I have never been offered coffee by a white lecturer. Except, of course, at job interviews.

Reading

    a   The Holy Bible: The King James Version
           (Oxford University Press)
           Jonah Chapter Two (Complete: Verses One to Nine)

A Light Outwith

3 March 2002

Last night I saw a television newsclip I did not see when it was transmitted years ago. In that sequence Margaret Thatcher said she offered "the proudest word in our language: Freeholder".

This greatly puzzled me. I have more reason than many to savor the word. Yet somehow, though the word is undoubtedly proud, or even vainglorious, it seemed to me she intended no literality.

I love my country, though I have never said a good word about it.

But it is the country of Langland and Mallory, of Shakespeare and Marlowe, Milton and Bunyan, Locke, Newton, Blake and Faraday, Mill, Russell, Ruskin and Arnold. And yes: Even of Darwin, Huxley, Hobbes and Spencer.

Lastly, because most memorably, it is the country of Martin, Wilberforce, Clarkson, Cooper and Fry.

We may disown the atheism of Darwin and Marlowe, the cold cynicism of Hobbes and denounce the condescending snobbery of Arnold. But these are our teachers. They have informed a modern world in which father and son have blazoned light and liberty across a planet.

And let us not forget teachers who chose not our tongue but our land. Our friend Voltaire, his compatriot Rousseau who penned his *Confessions* in Wootton Lodge, and that spent promethean and other anglophobe who wrote his three volumes of *Das Kapital* in Maitland Park.

Today a Catholic lit a candle in our midst and our chief elder, in a moving ministry on Holocaust Sunday, reminded us that our taper was not shrouded in barbed wire, for we enjoy amnesty denied elsewhere. But three hundred and thirty and more Quakers died captive, and it is because of such as she that the Light burns Free.

I am minded to dispute the choice of The Iron Lady. Should I choose "freedom" or "justice" as the proudest words in my language? Why should I parrot words I do not understand and cannot define? No. I nominate "candle".

For I remember that this gentle and luminous word was the parting gift of Latimer to his friend as the flames enveloped them both:-

*"**Be of good comfort, Master Ridley, and play the man; we shall this day light such a candle by God's Grace in England as I trust never shall be put out**"*[1].

Reference

1   "Foxe's Book of Martyrs"   (page 307)
           John Foxe   1563
           Ambassador Publications Limited of Belfast
           ISBN 1-898787-50-6

CHAPTER SIX

How to Cherish

5 December 2008

This is the counsel of a dying man. It is informed by the errors and depravities that took his mortal life a mortgage, and by the precepts of The Holy Bible.

Only love is important.

Though I am evil, I shall not betray you. For I have nothing to gain by misleading you, though good advice may win me Immortal Life.

We relate as individuals and yet are members of a collective. Therefore know and be loyal to several people rather than one ideology.

When a man or woman wants to be heard listen patiently, even when his anticipated message frustrates your urgent needs, or affronts your views. Favor him with your time, your prayers, your reassurance, and your kindly counsel. Be swift to love and slow to judge. Do not be soft with him but be kind and constructive. Respect his need for his honor and for your acceptance. Remember that the wages of war is common diminishment and the fruit of love mutual aggrandisement.

Love yourself a little but not too much. Others cherish you. If you are sick accept the best care and counsel with gratitude. Accept vital fluids or anaesthetic if needful: It is someone's mercy to you. Have a little alcohol or tobacco once in a while as your little treat, but do not betray yourself to habit or addiction for that is Gluttony that kills rather than cures. Take an intelligent interest in the world around you but do not obsess, neither be the toy of fad or fashion. If you exercise your brain, ply your body as much, and feed your soul. My Late Mother's last words to me were "keep on walking" and I intend to die afoot.

Respect your mother and father, and also any surrogate guardian who graced your childhood. Weigh their wisdom for yourself, but never argue or answer back. Let your gentle and dutiful answers be yes or no. You know that your parents will love you forever, and unconditionally. If you are adult, you also know that they have unresolved issues of their own that color their judgment, as does their natural reference to the mores of their youth.

Do not affront your body. It took Someone cleverer than you milliards of years to perfect. Can you enhance it? Have no tattoo or piercing made upon it. Do not commission plastic surgery or circumcision. Do not paint or powder it, or dye your hair or beard.

Wear enough but not too much. Dress decorously without show. The glint of gold is for The Cross of Christ or for your wedding band. You are the true treasure, beyond rubies. So uncover briskly and without shame, inciting no lust or lewd speculation.

Feed and water a little but not too much. Avoid psychotropic drugs including those doled out by governments as prophylaxis aimed at pandemic physical ills. Avoid pornography: It diverts your seed from its gainful target, and enfeebles what remains. Avoid self-indulgent or treacherous bedmates. They spread diseases that pollute the marriage bed, birthing weak generations who extinguish our species by default.

If as a man you take a woman cherish and protect her without deceit, for she will bear your child in pain and love, and needs you to help nurture him. Never withhold the sacred seed of life that is rightfully hers, or spend it fruitlessly. Help her keep her godly ways and will for both shall redound to your profit.

If as a woman you take a man honor him, and obey his every godly command without deceit. Keep your mind and tend your soul for they will profit your posterity. Your body is for your man and your child. Never withhold your sacred potential or frustrate its holy purpose, even when you think your time has passed.

If you beget a child demonstrate your love to him with steady constancy from his birth. Nurture and teach him with prayers and kisses and tender embraces. Praise his attainments and more especially his kindnesses, but not too much. Make your corrections brief and salutary but never humiliating, never in anger, and never to shame, always showing your love, your unwavering unconditional acceptance of him, and his rehabilitation. Lead him to love, and to take success and failure with cheer, and to covet nothing. At all costs, never banish him to dark places, literally or figuratively.

When feeble creatures trespass your land and property let them take their portion and raise their young in the sanctuary that you afford. Lay no trap or poison. If you hunt, shoot or fish see to it that your prey feeds your household and yourself. Remember that its demise is death to another family. Make sure that your prayer of thanksgiving reminds your loved ones of the fact. Otherwise, avoid meat. The human animal is a frugivore. Why abuse it with cruelty?

Find work that is honest and fulfilling rather than profitable or prestigious.

Never swear, take an oath, or wager. Never lend, borrow or speculate. Never do business in a house of God. If, however, you unfortunately fall into debt then seek with speed and candor to come to terms with your creditor. Ask for manageable incremental repayments, or better still discharge small debts with honest service.

Treat all courteously and fairly as equal fellows under God. Remember that the laws of man, juridical or scientific, change and decay. Render unto Caesar his due winnings, but despise the office not the man, for he is truly a reed blown by the wind, or rather a rootless weed in the fitful wrath of desiccating storms. Eschew politics. If you live in an absolute monarchy or a dictatorship take no part in sham elections or plebiscites. They mock the instruments of popular rule and hardly need your validation. This is no advocacy of a passive or unmanly servility. Quite the opposite. I tell you to be an active, helpful man or woman at the very van of progress. Endorse the leaders of your church or temple, mosque or meetinghouse. They know you and value your free approval. The best will repay fourfold, or broker a priceless prize.

Love without hate. Love your country and your people with cheerful kind regard to all others. Whatever your habits or assumptions treat individuals of any nation and any faith or none with fair amity. They do not belong to you. They are not yours to dispose of. They belong to Someone Else. He will put them in their place. Be ready to applaud the efforts and attainments of all and any. Eschew jealous rivalries and empty separatism. You are entitled to defend your family, your nation or yourself if life or liberty is in peril. But forgive your enemy as soon as he is no threat, and be merciful: You will win your most loyal friend. Many good men now dead forgave me my arrogance, my self-indulgence and my wickedness. I ask you to grant me no favors but instead to pass their godly clemencies onto the heads of others.

Except in extremis, avoid killing anything. It is a violation of God Himself. Do you carry a weapon? Do you use your vehicle as a weapon? Do not carry a weapon. The temptation to use it for its design purpose may be overwhelming. Do not pervert a tool except in the direst emergency.

Do not obtrude or assert a specious charity to salve your conscience or to purchase favor, giving with condescension and taking back with stealth. Rather befriend where you can, help the struggler with your love and service, and permit a free spirit to move forward revitalised.

Walk with God. Walk with God and keep on praying. Help any sorry creatures along your path with kind indulgence and lasting works. That way you will be happy, healthy and wise and your posterity shall prosper.

This is more and better than I did.

It is enough.

www.ingramcontent.com/pod-product-compliance
Lightning Source LLC
Chambersburg PA
CBHW050805220426
43209CB00088BA/1647